# American Steam
## volume 2

*Robert A. LeMassena*

Rolling downgrade at 60 mph., one of the Erie's heavy USRA 4-6-2's was leaning into the 5°30' S-curve, having six inches super-elevation, at Hillburn, New York. These powerful locomotives hauled all of the railroad's first-class passenger trains between Jersey City, New Jersey, and Chicago. [R. A. LeMassena]

# American Steam

### BY ROBERT A. LE MASSENA

### LOCOMOTIVES OF THE NORTHEAST

**Front Cover Caption**
Howard Fogg's beautiful watercolor painting shows Delaware, Lackawanna & Western engine No. 1154 ascending the 1.7-percent grade eastward from Scranton, Pennsylvania. Despite their 80-inch drivers, these huge 4-6-4's could take 10 heavy passenger cars up the hill without a helper.

## LOCOMOTIVES OF THE NORTHEAST

**SUNDANCE** PUBLICATIONS Ltd.
250 BROADWAY, DENVER, COLORADO 80203

Published by
Sundance Publications, Ltd., Denver, Colorado

Graphical Presentation and Printing by
Sundance Publications, Ltd., Denver, Colorado

Binding by
Hawley Bookbinding Co., Denver, Colorado

Typesetting by
Russ Collman and LaserWriting, Inc.
Denver, Colorado

*Production Manager – Dell A. McCoy*
*Director of Photography – Steven J. Meyers*
*Editorial Assistant – Gary D. Anderson*

Copyright © 1989 by Sundance Publications, Ltd.
Denver, Colorado 80203. Printed in U.S.A.
All rights reserved. This book, or parts thereof,
may not be reproduced in any form without
written permission of the publisher.

First Printing of Volume 2: May 1989
ISBN 0-913582-05-0

Robert A. LeMassena, Author

— NOTE —

In conformance with the notations used in *Articulated Steam Locomotives of North America* (Sundance Publications, Limited, 1979), the "+" symbol has been used to designate the point-of-articulation in wheel arrangements: 2-8+8-2 for a Mallet, or 2-6+4T for a Fairlie locomotive.

# Introduction

BECAUSE VOLUME I of *American Steam* was primarily the work of a single photographer, Ben Cutler, the scope of its contents was limited to those railroads within range of his home in southeastern Ohio, plus several other railroads encountered on his trips to the Pacific Coast. Consequently, there was no photographic representation of railroading in the northeastern section of the nation. A line drawn from Cleveland, Ohio, to Pittsburgh, Pennsylvania, and thence to Cumberland, Maryland, and Richmond, Virginia, marked the eastern boundary of Ben Cutler's photographic territory.

This enormous void has been filled to a great extent by the work of two other photographers, whose homes were in central Ohio and northern New Jersey. There are some gaps in coverage, however, largely due to the restrictions accompanying World War II, as well as the difficulty of reaching Maine (for example) over a weekend. This accounts for the absence of such notable railroads as the Maine Central, Bangor & Aroostook, Grand Trunk, and the Rutland. The Reading and the Pennsylvania–Reading Seashore Lines could be covered adequately only from a base in Philadelphia, but the many interesting railroads in western Pennsylvania could be approached from Ohio. Yet, the Detroit, Toledo & Ironton is among the missing, despite its proximity.

The territorial overlap within Ben Cutler's province has provided the opportunity to expand upon his pictorial coverage in that area; and the railroad overlap south of the Mason–Dixon Line has been utilized to demonstrate the remarkable variety of steam locomotives which worked in that region.

In several instances it has been possible to assemble rather complete photographic rosters of a railroad's motive power, with emphasis given to examples of the lesser-known, though not at all less interesting, locomotives. It is believed that some of the railroads, and several of the locomotives, have not been illustrated in any previous publication.

Because new locomotives possessed a special appeal due to their novelty or great size, modified, rebuilt and second-hand engines have been photographically neglected. In this volume, however, almost half of the photographs illustrate interesting modifications made to the original locomotive, and a substantial proportion show remarkable mechanical transformations of boilers, machinery and tenders. It was not possible for the two photographers to supply all of the desired pictures; so, Harold K. Vollrath of Kansas City, Missouri, generously supplied what was needed from his extensive collection.

It should be recalled that most of these photographs were taken in an era prior to the common usage of automobiles. Railroad photographers rode passenger trains to lineside locations, and then walked long distances to suitable sites for photographs. They also rode on electric streetcars, interurban cars, bicycles, motorcycles, and even busses. A photographer's range was limited to whatever he could reach in a day, or in a weekend, and many an excursion produced only eight or ten exposures. Most of the cameras used large size black-and-white roll film with a maximum speed of ASA 100. The 35 mm. camera, then a rather primitive affair, used color-transparency film of no more than ASA 10 to begin with.

Railroad photography was considered to be a highly suspicious activity during World War II years (1941–1945, and even during the "Cold War" years following the war, as was taking pictures in an engine terminal at any time. At other times and places, photographers have been questioned by both railroad police and local police officers. In view of these handicaps and impediments, it is indeed most remarkable that so many excellent photographs of locomotives and trains were taken.

The arrival of the Lackawanna's first diesel-electric freight-service units in 1945–1946 released several 4-8-4's, which displaced the 4-8-2's and early 4-8-4's on passenger trains. In this panorama of the westbound *Lackawanna Limited* near Cresco, Pennsylvania, No. 1610 was helping the 1635 up the 1.7-percent grade. [W. R. Osborne]

# TABLE OF CONTENTS

## NEW ENGLAND
| | |
|---|---|
| *Barre & Chelsea* | *10* |
| *Boston & Albany* | *10* |
| *Boston & Maine* | *14* |
| *Central Vermont* | *19* |
| *Mount Washington* | *26* |
| *New York, New Haven & Hartford* | *22* |
| *Portland Terminal* | *27* |
| *Rutland* | *27* |

## MIDDLE ATLANTIC REGION
| | |
|---|---|
| *Brooklyn Dock & Terminal* | *32* |
| *Central of New Jersey* | *30* |
| *Delaware & Hudson* | *33* |
| *Delaware, Lackawanna & Western* | *39* |
| *Erie* | *62* |
| *Harlem Transfer* | *69* |
| *Lehigh & Hudson River* | *70* |
| *Lehigh & New England* | *71* |
| *Lehigh Valley* | *74* |
| *Morristown & Erie* | *79* |
| *New York Central* | *79* |
| *New York, Ontario & Western* | *92* |
| *Toronto, Hamilton & Buffalo* | *93* |

## COMMONWEALTH OF PENNSYLVANIA
| | |
|---|---|
| *Alan Wood Steel* | *96* |
| *Baltimore & Ohio* | *96* |
| *Monongahela* | *117* |
| *Montour* | *120* |
| *Pennsylvania* | *122* |
| *Pennsylvania Power & Light* | *140* |
| *Pittsburgh & Lake Erie* | *138* |
| *Pittsburgh & West Virginia* | *141* |
| *Upper Merion & Plymouth* | *144* |
| *Western Maryland* | *144* |

## BEYOND THE APPALACHIANS
| | |
|---|---|
| *Akron, Canton & Youngstown* | *152* |
| *Alton* | *153* |
| *Alton & Southern* | *154* |
| *Belt Railway of Chicago* | *156* |
| *Chicago & Calumet Terminal* | *156* |
| *Chicago & Illinois Midland* | *157* |
| *Grand Trunk Western* | *160* |
| *Illinois Central* | *162* |
| *Illinois Midland* | *157* |
| *New York, Chicago & St. Louis* | *171* |
| *River Terminal* | *176* |
| *Wabash* | *176* |
| *Wheeling & Lake Erie* | *181* |

## NORTHERN SOUTHLAND
| | |
|---|---|
| *Chesapeake & Ohio* | *195* |
| *Clinchfield* | *190* |
| *East Tennessee & Western North Carolina* | *213* |
| *Interstate* | *211* |
| *Norfolk Southern* | *213* |
| *Norfolk & Western* | *214* |
| *Tennessee & North Carolina* | *237* |
| *Virginian* | *234* |
| *Winston-Salem Southbound* | *243* |

## MISCELLANEOUS
| | |
|---|---|
| *Duluth, Missabe & Iron Range* | *245* |
| *U.S. Army Transportation Corps* | *253* |

# Chapter I

## NEW ENGLAND

Barre & Chelsea
Boston & Albany
Boston & Maine
Central Vermont
Mount Washington
New York, New Haven & Hartford
Portland Terminal
Rutland

Because New England's six states were almost isolated by the Hudson River and Lake Champlain valleys, its railroads were localized in character. The Boston & Albany was a rather independent element of the New York Central System, and its locomotives followed NYC designs, though modified to surmount the Berkshire Hills in western Massachusetts where the first 2-8-4 was tested to demonstrate its superior performance. Much of the Boston & Maine's trackage was in New Hampshire, with very little in Maine. Its east-west mainline penetrated the hills of western Massachusetts with the five-mile Hoosac Tunnel, through which electric locomotives pulled both steam engines and cars. Central Vermont was the Canadian National's subsidiary, which connected Montreal with New London, Connecticut, on Long Island Sound. Its principle obstacle was the bi-directional climb over Vermont's Green Mountains, an operation which utilized the nation's smallest 2-10-4's and hand-fired 4-8-2's. Connecticut's rail transport was dominated by the New Haven's network of branches and affiliated local transit lines. Its enormous passenger and freight traffic was hauled by all-electric motive power between New York and New Haven, Connecticut, after 1905, but steam remained dominant elsewhere on its system. The Mount Washington Railway, which ascended Mount Washington, New Hampshire, to its 6,288-foot summit, used the Marsh type of cog-wheel propulsion. It was the first such installation in North America, and the terminus was the highest railroad location east of the Rocky Mountains. The remoteness of coal supplies and the advanced age of steam locomotives, very few of which were constructed after 1937, caused New England's railroads to convert to diesel-electric propulsion at an early date; and by 1952, an operating steam locomotive was a rare sight indeed.

The B&A's 1.5-percent grades eastward over the Berkshire Mountains from Selkirk, New York, was the proving ground for Lima's revolutionary 2-8-4, which combined large grate area and high steam pressure to attain greater power with decreased fuel consumption. Between 1926 and 1930, the B&A bought 55 similar engines from Lima. In this steamy panorama, the 1437 and 1417, with wide-open throttles and boosters working, were assaulting the hill near the summit. [Unknown]

The Barre & Chelsea's trackage, located in and around marble quarries in Vermont, was both steep and sharply curved. Consequently, it employed an uncommon locomotive, the 0-6-2T, like No. 6, built by Baldwin in 1912. [I. W. Saunders]

In the early 1900's, the Boston & Albany purchased 18 bi-directional 2-6-6T engines for its Boston commuter service. This one was No. 309, awaiting a trip out of South Station in 1939. [R. A. LeMassena]

Resembling the earlier New York Central 4-6-4's, the Boston & Albany's engines had smaller drivers and eight-wheel tenders. The last ten were built by Lima in 1931. [R. A. LeMassena]

Increased commuter traffic in Boston caused the B&A to acquire five large 4-6-6T's from American in 1928. They were operated at high speeds in either direction. [Unknown]

Because of its mainline grades, the Boston & Albany acquired 4–6–2's with smaller drivers and larger cylinders than similar locomotives operated on the New York Central System. The unusual placement of the air pump was unique to these engines. [H. K. Vollrath Collection]

For a period of 14 years, the 2–8–2, identical to those built for the New York Central, was the B&A's standard freight locomotive. When they were displaced by 2–8–4's in the mid-1920's, many of them, like No. 1203, were modified for local freight service. [H. K. Vollrath Collection]

Even though the B&A had acquired powerful 2-8-4's by 1930, it continued to use its slow-moving 2-6+6-2's on unscheduled freight trains. The 12 engines like No. 1301 were built to handle the extra traffic produced by World War I. [H. K. Vollrath Collection]

All but two of the B&A's 2-8-4's, Numbers 1423 and 1434, were scrapped. Equipped with 12-wheel tenders from NYC 4-6-4's, they became Tennessee, Alabama & Georgia Numbers 601 and 602. [H. K. Vollrath Collection]

The Boston & Maine is well remembered for its usage of ancient 2-6-0's for branchline passenger and freight service until 1956; and many of them had worked for 50 years with only minor mechanical modifications. When these little engines vanished, so did the track upon which they ran. [H. K. Vollrath Collection]

Mainline passenger trains were pulled by a fleet of 90 light 4-6-2's, constructed between 1910 and 1916; another 10 were acquired in 1923. But, when new locomotives could not be obtained during World War II, the B&M bought four freight-service 4-6-2's from the Delaware, Lackawanna & Western, and operated them for another 10 years. [H. K. Vollrath Collection]

The 10 4-6-2's, erected by Lima in 1934 and 1937, were among the heaviest and most powerful of their type. They weighed 340,000 pounds, had 80-inch drivers and were equipped with trailing-truck boosters. [R. A. LeMassena]

The Boston & Maine's fleet of 0-8-0 switchers, 22 from American and 15 from Baldwin, was quite small for a large railroad. All of them were constructed between 1922 and 1929, and this photograph, taken at Greenfield, Massachusetts, shows that they also worked in local freight service. [R. A. LeMassena]

Over an interval of only five years, the B&M acquired a fleet of more than 250 2-8-0's, the last 25, numbered 2710–2734, having been delivered from American in 1916. Modifications included superheaters and feedwater heaters, which enabled these locomotives to handle local freights into the mid-1950's. [R. A. LeMassena]

Until the arrival of 25 2-8-4's from Lima in 1928 and 1929, the B&M did not have any fast-freight locomotives. All of the new engines had trailing-truck boosters and Coffin feedwater heaters, and the last five came with 12-wheel tenders. In this scene at North Adams, Massachusetts, the 4009 and its westbound train had just been hauled through the Hoosac Tunnel by electric locomotives. [R. A. LeMassena]

After its experience with the successful 2-8-4's, the B&M reverted to an older concept — the 4-8-2 — when it needed more modern locomotives. Although the 18 such engines delivered from Baldwin during 1935–1941 were among the heaviest of that wheel arrangement, they had only 80 percent of the grate area of the previous type. But with larger drivers, they could be assigned to passenger service. The final five were equipped with enormous 4-10 tenders, and they were retained in 1947, when the first 13 were sold to the Baltimore and Ohio. [R. A. LeMassena]

Whereas most 2-10-2's were designed with the firebox behind the drivers and supported by the trailing truck, the B&M's locomotives placed the firebox above the rear drivers, thus restricting steam production. Ten out of the original 30 engines were rebuilt in 1940 and renumbered, as illustrated by the 2906, enroute to Rotterdam Junction, New York. [R. A. LeMassena]

The B&M's oil-burning 2-6+6-2's lasted only a year before being sold to the Maine Central. They were acquired to help trains through the long Hoosac Tunnel, but the bore was electrified in mid-1911, eliminating the articulated helpers. [H. K. Vollrath Collection]

The railroad's only other articulateds were a pair of ponderous 0-8+8-0's, numbered 800 and 801, which worked for seven years on the hump in the yard at Mechanicville, New York. In 1929 they were sold to the Utah Copper Company. [H. K. Vollrath Collection]

Whenever the Central Vermont's 4-6-2's were not available, the railroad utilized one of its elderly 4-6-0's to escort its mainline passenger trains between St. Albans, Vermont, and Montreal, Ontario, Canada. This consist was the southbound Ambassador at East Swanton, Vermont. [R. A. LeMassena]

The Canadian National operated its 4-8-4's, like the 6131, from Montreal to St. Albans, double-heading with a Central Vermont 2-8-0 whenever the tonnage was excessive. These smaller engines were standard freight power south of Brattleboro, Vermont. [R. A. LeMassena]

When the railroad's four 4-8-2's were delivered in 1927, they were not equipped with mechanical stokers, a deficiency which curtailed their power on the steep grades over the Green Mountains. They were assigned to the *Montrealer/Washingtonian,* engine No. 601, between Springfield, Massachusetts, and Montreal, Ontario, and the *Ambassador,* engine No. 603, between Montreal and White River Junction, Vermont. [R. A. LeMassena]

Because the Central Vermont belonged to Canadian National Railways, the CV's 10 2-10-4's were the largest two-cylinder locomotives in the British Commonwealth. American built them in 1927 to replace double-headed 2-8-0's, though sometimes trains were so heavy that they were themselves double-headed southbound from St. Albans. All of them had trailing-truck boosters and an extra-wide frame around the trailing truck, like that on CNR 4-8-4's. [R. A. LeMassena]

The New York, New Haven & Hartford's usual motive power for passenger trains was the 4-6-2, 38 of which were delivered between 1907 and 1913. One-hundred more, numbered 1300–1399, had arrived by 1916. The 1391 shows little change, except for the Elesco feedwater heater, headlight and 12-wheel tender for *Yankee Clipper* service. [H. W. Pontin]

Heavier consists, faster speeds and considerable curvature in the New York–Boston mainline were the reasons for the New Haven's acquisition of 10 Baldwin 4-6-4's in 1937. Numbered 1400–1409, they were the last steam locomotives purchased by the railroad. [H. W. Pontin]

Somewhat later than most railroads, the NYNH&H obtained its first 2–8–2's in 1916, 33 of them from American. Those numbered 3000–3024 were not very large; they weighed the same as the railroad's 4–6–2's. Too light for heavy mainline service, they were soon superseded by 4–8–2's. [H. K. Vollrath Collection]

A group of 165 0-6-0's, built between 1902 and 1910, had become inadequate to handle the heavier trains after World War I; so the railroad augmented their ranks with 35 USRA-style 0-8-0's from American between 1920 and 1922. Sixteen additional 0-8-0's, huge three-cylinder engines, were added in 1924 and 1927. The 3608, seen here at Campbell Hall, New York, had come over from the freight yard at Maybrook to deliver and pick up cars. [R. A. LeMassena]

Following the practice of the New York Central, the New Haven began to assemble a fleet of 4-8-2's for mainline freight service by buying 49 USRA standard light 4-8-2's from American in 1919–1924. Their 69-inch driving wheels enabled them to handle heavy passenger trains, as the 3333 was doing at Springfield, Massachusetts. The engine had been modified by the application of a new trailing truck and a feedwater heater. The last 16 engines were given the 6-6 cylindrical tenders, which had accompanied the three-cylinder 0-8-0's in 1924–1927. [R. A. LeMassena, H. K. Vollrath Collection]

The New Haven was satisfied enough with its 4-8-2's that it ordered eight improved models, receiving one, No. 3500, in 1924 and seven in 1926. They were equipped with a front-end throttle, an Elesco feedwater heater, Southern-type valve gear, a McClellan water-tube firebox and an eight-wheel tender. The fireboxes were unsatisfactory; so, the boilers were rebuilt with radial-stay fireboxes. At the same time, Walschaerts valve gear replaced the Southern type; an additional compressor was installed; and the tender was enlarged, riding on six-wheel trucks. [R. A. LeMassena]

In 1926 and 1928, the railroad received a total of 13 three-cylinder 4-8-2's, numbered 3550–3562. As was customary with American's locomotives, the outside cylinders had Walschaerts valve gear, while the valve for the inner one was actuated by Gresley valve gear mounted on the pilot. [H. K. Vollrath Collection]

The 50 2-10-2's received in 1918 were the result of a new president's philosophy (from the Santa Fé system). At first, they were utilized on any mainline, but operational problems at higher speeds caused them to be assigned between New Haven, Connecticut, and Maybrook, New York. No. 3208 has received an Elesco feedwater heater, and its smokebox has been recessed for the future installation of two compound air pumps on the pilot. The inside-bearing trailing truck was never changed. [R. A. LeMassena]

Until 1969, when the Mount Washington Railway completed locomotive No. 10 in its own shops, No. 9, built by the American Locomotive Company in 1908, was the railroad's newest motive power. Each pair of front or back cylinders drove a transverse shaft through gears, and that shaft was geared to the traction pinion-gear engaging the rack. [H. K. Vollrath Collection]

When the Maine Central converted its passenger service to diesel-electric operation in 1953, it sold one of its two Baldwin (1930) 4-6-4's to its Portland Terminal subsidiary, which used it for another five years before modifying it, as did the MC, for snow-removal work. [H. K. Vollrath Collection]

Constructed by American in 1946, Rutland 4-8-2's, numbered 90–93, were the last such commercially built locomotives in the U.S.A. Provided with 73-inch drivers, the same as those used on the railroad's heavy 4-6-2's, they were capable of handling both passenger and freight trains. Unhappily, they worked for only six years before having been retired in favor of internal-combustion motive power. [Ralph Phillips]

Leading the eastbound *Pocono Express,* DL&W 4-6-4 No. 1153 roars through East Orange, New Jersey, at 60 mph., precisely on time. Its green flags indicated that an advance section of the *Lackawanna Limited* would be following four hours later. [R. A. LeMassena]

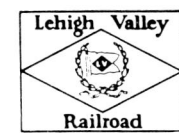

# Chapter II

## MIDDLE ATLANTIC REGION

*Brooklyn Dock & Terminal*
*Central of New Jersey*
*Delaware & Hudson*
*Delaware, Lackawanna & Western*
*Erie*
*Harlem Transfer*
*Lehigh & Hudson River*
*Lehigh & New England*
*Lehigh Valley*
*Morristown & Erie*
*New York Central*
*New York, Ontario & Western*
*Toronto, Hamilton & Buffalo*

Surrounded by New England, Canada, the Atlantic Ocean and the northern end of the Appalachian Mountains, the Middle Atlantic Region was covered with a dense network of railroads. One common commodity was hard coal mined in eastern Pennsylvania. This was the principal source of traffic for the Central of New Jersey; Delaware & Hudson; Delaware, Lackawanna & Western; Erie; Lehigh & Hudson River; Lehigh & New England; Lehigh Valley, and New York, Ontario & Western. However, that coal, routed to cities along the Atlantic coast, had to surmount as least one mountain ridge, whose grades, though short, were steep. Double-headers and triple-pushers were daily events. Only the Reading, and Delaware & Hudson used Mallets, though the Erie experimented with them for a few years. Surprisingly, the Central of New Jersey; Delaware, Lackawanna & Western, and Lehigh & Hudson River did not utilize locomotives with more than four driving axles. The 4-6-2 was the universal passenger-service engine, and many of them were very heavy examples. The DL&W was the first one to use 4-8-2's and 4-8-4's on passenger trains, and the only one to use a large number of three-cylinder engines (4-8-2's) in freight service until their replacement by diesel-electric units. Originally, the locomotives were constructed with very large grate areas, so that hard coal could be burned. Then, when that fuel became more costly, soft coal was burned; and, the newer locomotives were built with normally proportioned fireboxes. Only the New York Central possessed a "water-level" route between New York City and Buffalo, New York, and its four-track mainline carried an enormous passenger and freight traffic, hauled by modern 4-6-4's, 4-8-2's and 4-8-4's. Despite its great fleet of locomotives, some of which had been delivered as late as 1948, steam vanished from the NYC in late 1956. The Pennsylvania, however, continued to operate steam locomotives in both passenger and freight service until the end of 1957, long after almost all other neighboring railroads had converted to internal-combustion motive power.

The Central of New Jersey's 21 4-6-2's were notable for their 84-square-foot grate area, because they burned a mixture of hard and soft coal. Also, they were among the heaviest of their type, 334,000 pounds for the 810–814 group, which had 74-inch drivers for service on the mainlines in Pennsylvania. The 831–835 group had 79-inch drivers for fast passenger runs on lines in New Jersey. [W. B. Crater, R. A. LeMassena]

For its commuter service out of Jersey City, New Jersey, the CNJ utilized a fleet of antiquated center-cab 4-6-0's, some second-hand 2-6-2 tank engines and six 4-6-4T's constructed by Baldwin in 1923, numbered 225–230. [I. W. Saunders]

Patterned after the USRA's heavy 2-8-2, the CNJ's version was embellished with an extra-large firebox, having a 95-square-foot grate area. Some of them were improved with cast trailing-truck frames, feedwater heaters and 21,000-gallon tenders. The 933 was among the newest, from Baldwin in 1925. [R. A. LeMassena]

The CNJ's biggest switchers were 0-8-0's numbered 315–324, erected by Baldwin in 1930. No one could miss their large tenders, oversized fireboxes and front-end throttles, but only one small airpump. [H. K. Vollrath Collection]

The Brooklyn Dock & Terminal was a Delaware, Lackawanna & Western subsidiary, whose lone locomotive, No. 2, was added to the DL&W's roster in 1914, and bore the number "8" thereafter, although its operating area remained unchanged. [Baldwin Locomotive Works]

Delaware & Hudson locomotives were notable for their bulging Wootten fireboxes, to burn hard coal, and the British influence on the styling following a rebuilding. These ex-center-cab 4-4-0's were used on short local and branch runs. [H. K. Vollrath Collection]

Center-cab 4-6-0's were rebuilt into rather nice-looking engines for light passenger service on the Delaware & Hudson mainlines. [H. K. Vollrath Collection]

One of the 4-6-2's, No. 653, constructed in the railroad's shops, was rebuilt with rotary-cam valve gear, and its steam pressure was increased to 325 psi. in 1934. Neither modification appeared to be particularly successful, although the locomotive remained in service until 1951. [H. K. Vollrath Collection]

The 15 D&H 4-8-4's, purchased in 1943, were intended for heavy passenger service or fast freight trains. Unfortunately, they worked for only 10 years before being displaced by diesel-electric units. [C. W. Burns]

Ignoring all other wheel arrangements until 1940, the D&H developed the 2-8-0 extensively, and this type of locomotive attained engine weights of 300,000 pounds. The final group, with boilers made by American, were constructed in the railroad's shops during 1927–1930, and they were numbered 1111–1122. No. 1113 was assisting a 4-6+6-4, three cars back, at Willow Glen, New York. [R. A. LeMassena]

All of the railroad's 0-8-0 switchers were fabricated from center-cab 2-8-0's, which had become inadequate for mainline service. [H. K. Vollrath Collection]

Spaced three years apart, beginning in 1924, American erected three experimental 2-8-0's for the D&H, all having water-tube fireboxes and increasing steam pressure, 350, 400 and 500 psi. And they were exceptionally heavy, 348,000, 337,000 and 356,000 pounds. All were cross compounds, with tender-truck boosters to augment their 72,000-pound tractive effort. Excessive maintenance caused them to be retired in 1935. [Three photos: H. K. Vollrath Collection]

The ultimate experimental fiasco was No. 1403, a four-cylinder, 500 psi., triple-expansion 4-8-0 delivered by American in 1933. It weighed 382,000 pounds, and theoretically could exert a 110,000-pound drawbar pull, using high-pressure steam in all cylinders, and with its tender booster working. It never made a successful trip and was retired in 1935, after having been operated less than 10,000 miles. [H. K. Vollrath Collection]

The D&H's 13 0-8+8-0 Mallets were among the first to have been built, 1910–1912. They had tiny drivers (51 inches), enormous low-pressure cylinders (41 inches) and large fireboxes (100 square feet). They were good for only one service, slow-speed helper duty. Then, commencing in 1930, the railroad rebuilt one each year in a most unusual manner. The steam pressure was increased to compensate for the increase in driver diameter (245 psi. and 57 inches respectively) The cylinders were reduced to 40 inches, but the stroke was increased from 28 to 30 inches. When they were retired, circa 1950, a total of nine had been modified. [H. K. Vollrath Collection]

By 1940, the D&H's 13 0-8+8-0 helpers, delivered 1910–1912, were both overloaded and insufficient to cope with pre-war traffic surges. Consequently, 40 single-expansion 4-6+6-4's were acquired between 1940 and 1942 to handle line-haul freight, thus releasing 2-8-0's for helper duty. However, they were frequently used as helpers when other locomotives were not available. Diesel-electrics replaced them in 1953. [C. W. Burns]

The Delaware, Lackawanna & Western owned only two 0-4-0T engines. No. 7, delivered by Baldwin in 1922, worked in the locomotive shops at Scranton, Pennsylvania. [E. L. May]

Until they were replaced by huge 0-8-0's in the 1930's, the 0-6-0 was the common yard switcher for the DL&W. No. 142 was one of the last ones delivered by American in 1910, and it was not scrapped until 1945. [J. P. Ahrens]

In 1928, after the big 4-8-4's began to arrive, the railroad found that it needed a larger shop switcher at Scranton. So, they took a 1908-model 0-6-0, No. 120, and converted it into this unique tank engine. [W. R. Osborne]

The 987 had been built in 1901 by American as a center-cab engine; then, in 1937 (when this photograph was taken), it was rebuilt as shown in this portrait. However, it was retired after working only three years in branch-line service. [F. H. Donahue]

One of the rebuilt 4-4-0's, No. 988, received semi-streamlining treatment in 1938. In this scene at Hoboken, it was hauling a Boonton Line local passenger train. [R. A. LeMassena]

Although the 66 DL&W 2-6-0's had been constructed between 1903 and 1911, they were modified with Walschaerts valve gear and contemporary standard appliances. The 535 (built in 1911), pulling a Hoboken–Secaucus shop train in 1936, lasted only two more years. No. 566 (built in 1908), on a local freight at Binghamton, New York, in 1947, worked another 10 years before being scrapped. [J. P. Ahrens, E. L. May]

A total of nine 4-6-0's, built between 1905 and 1910, were converted in the railroad's shops from center-cab engines to the usual type in 1938. They were used in commuter service and for accommodation trains on the line through Paterson, New Jersey. No. 1011 was given the semi-streamlined cosmetic treatment, also. Replaced by 4-6-2's, all of them were scrapped during 1942. [R. A. LeMassena, J. P. Ahrens]

The Lackawanna's 4–6–2's were provided with three driver diameters, examples of which are shown here — 73 inches on No. 1114 for commuter and local passenger trains; 79 inches on No. 1120 for mainline passenger service; and 70 inches on No. 1193 for fast freight trains. The 1114 worked for 33 years, and the last four freight models were sold to the Boston & Maine in 1943, after 18 years of service. The 1120 remained active, often double-heading with 1500-series 4–8–4's on the Lackawanna Limited, until the end of mainline steam operations in 1953, accumulating three decades of use. [Two upper photos: R. A. LeMassena, lower photo: H. K. Vollrath Collection]

The Lackawanna system had a large number of center-cab 4–4–0's, which were used in commuter service at Hoboken, New Jersey, and on some branchlines. Nine of the newest ones were rebuilt with Baker valve motion and conventional cabs during 1937–1938. The 978 was at Washington, New Jersey, in 1945, handling a typical local train. [R. A. LeMassena]

During 1939, the Delaware, Lackawanna & Western's No. 1151 was temporarily renumbered "1939" for a part it played in the New York Worlds Fair, and this heavy 4–6–4 was modified again for the 1940 fair, as this view portrays. [T. T. Taber]

Four of the 4–6–2's having 79-inch drivers, Numbers 1115, 1117, 1123 and 1136, were given a "streamlined" modification in 1938. The 1117 was photographed double-heading with 4–6–4 No. 1153 on the westbound *Lackawanna Limited* at Scranton. No. 1123 and its tender were painted with red, white and green trim. [W. R. Osbore, T. T. Taber]

The Lackawanna's last steam locomotives were five 4–6–4's erected by American in 1937. They were slightly larger than the New York Central's 4–6–4's, but somewhat less powerful. They replaced 4–6–2's on mainline passenger trains between Scranton and Buffalo, New York, while the spare engine made a round trip to Hoboken. No. 1151, shown renumbered "1939" for the 1939 World's Fair, was modified for its appearance at the fair. The 1155 and 1939 were photographed at East Orange, New Jersey, with the eastbound *Pocono Express* [Both views: R. A. LeMassena]

During World War II the oldest freight-service 4–8–4's were equipped with a compound air-compressor, mounted on the pilot deck, and a Worthington feedwater heater was placed ahead of the stack. Afterwards, displaced by diesel-electric units, they handled passenger trains which had been hauled by 4–8–2's. This one was the westbound *Chicago Limited* at East Orange, New Jersey. [R. A. LeMassena]

Big 0-8-0 switchers were used in major freight yards on the system, but two of them, 198 and 199, were built with very large cylinders specifically for the hump yards at Scranton, Pennsylvania, and Secaucus, New Jersey. These older engines remained in service despite the addition of 60 "new" ones between 1929 and 1935. Instead of acquiring USRA duplicates, the Lackawanna's shops used 38 obsolete freight 4-6-2's and 22 older 2-8-2's for these locomotives. Having large cylinders and drivers (58 inches), they replaced 2-8-0's in local freight service. No. 232 was the last steam locomotive in service on the DL&W, being removed from the roster in 1954. [C. T. Andrews, W. S. Kuba]

Between 1901 and 1910, the Lackawanna purchased nearly 200 2-8-0's, split almost evenly between the 300 series, with wide fireboxes, and the 700 series, with normal-width fireboxes. Otherwise, they were essentially identical, and they were standard freight power until the mid-1930's, when greatly reduced traffic and the construction of 0-8-0's caused them to be scrapped. [Unknown, E. L. May]

In the spring of 1939 4-8-4 No. 1504 escorted a railfan trip from Hoboken, New Jersey, to Scranton, Pennsylvania. In this scene, the train had paused atop the lofty Paulins Kill Viaduct on the Lackawanna Cutoff. [R. A. LeMassena]

DL&W 2-8-2's came in two sizes, heavy (Numbers 1201–1262) and heavier (Numbers 2101–2150). The last 10, constructed by American in 1924, were heavier than those of the Chesapeake & Ohio. The first 27 engines had inside-bearing trailing trucks and Walschaerts valve gear; the remaining 1200's had Baker gear and Cole trailing trucks. The 1261 was the only DL&W locomotive equipped with an Elesco feedwater heater. All of the 2100's had Baker gear and trailing-truck boosters. After the 4-8-4's arrived, the first 22 2-8-2's were rebuilt into 0-8-0 switchers, and the 2100's worked on local freights and as helpers, as illustrated by the 2130 assisting 4-8-4 No. 1608 at Mount Pocono, Pennsylvania. [H. K. Vollrath Collection, unknown, R. A. LeMassena]

The railroad's first five 4-8-2's were duplicates of the USRA's standard heavy design, constructed by American in 1924. Equipped with Baker valve gear originally, they were modified for Walschaerts gear in 1930. Three years before its sale to the Atlantic Coast Line in 1943, the 1402 was photographed at West End, New Jersey. The ACL modified the five DL&W 4-8-2's by adding a Worthington feedwater heater, compound airpump, and extra coal space on the tenders. Five more 4-8-2's with three cylinders, 1450–1454, arrived in 1925. They had larger drivers, larger fireboxes and greater weight. After only five years of service, they were rebuilt with two cylinders having a longer stroke, and greater steam pressure. The 1454 was steaming through Paterson, New Jersey, at the head of the eastbound Pocono Express when this portrait was made. [Upper photos: R. A. LeMassena, lower photo: H. K. Vollrath Collection]

Included in the Lackawanna's roster were 35 brutish three-cylinder 4-8-2's weighing almost 400,000 pounds and equipped with trailing-truck boosters, which gave them a drawbar-pull of almost 100,000 pounds. They were delivered during 1926–1927, and were used almost exclusively on coal trains between Wilkes-Barre, Pennsylvania, and Secaucus, New Jersey, until their retirement in 1946–1949. This one was the 2230, westbound with empties at Paterson, New Jersey. [R. A. LeMassena]

The DL&W's first 4-8-4's were among the very earliest of that wheel arrangement, and also among the very last locomotives built at American's Brooks Works (1927). Larger in every respect than the 4-8-2's, they were given quite big drivers — 77 inches — for heavy passenger service between Hoboken and Scranton, yet they were not equipped with trailing-truck boosters. Shown in its original form, No. 1502 was emerging from the eastern portal of the double tunnels at Hoboken. In the late 1930's, they were rebuilt with one-piece cast-steel beds and were equipped with two compound compressors, as illustrated by the 1501 at Orange, New Jersey. [T. A. Gay, R. A. LeMassena]

So pleased was the railroad with its passenger-service 4-8-4's that two years later it ordered 20 more with 70-inch drivers for fast freight service. They used the same boiler, supported by a one-piece cast-steel bed, which included the steam delivery piping to the cylinders. Despite their 12-wheel tenders, the locomotive wheelbase was only two feet longer. No. 1620 is seen roaring westward through Denville, New Jersey, in 1939, just a couple of years before it was modified, as were all others, like the 1610 with a Worthington feedwater heater and a compound airpump mounted on the pilot. It was double-heading with another 4-8-4, No. 1634, at Mount Pocono, Pennsylvania. [R. A. LeMassena, W. R. Osborne]

Shortly after its delivery in 1932, 4-8-4 No. 1622 was ascending the 1.7-percent grade westbound at Mount Pocono, Pennsylvania. It was assisted by one of the DL&W's heavy 2-8-2's pushing behind the caboose. [Unknown]

The 4-8-4's were so superior to the 2-8-2's in freight service that 20 more were ordered in 1934. Actually, they were dual-service engines, having been given 74-inch drivers. Their boilers were again redesigned internally to increase steam production, and the longer wheelbase was kept within the 90-foot turntable limit. The 1641 was hauling an eastbound perishable consist through Paterson in 1940. Two other views show two sections of the eastbound *Lackawanna Limited* departing Scranton, Pennsylvania, in 1938, with 1647 and 1505 on the first section and 1650 and 1643 pulling the all-coach second section. [Upper view: R. A. LeMassena, other views: W. R. Osborne]

No. 90 was a typical example of the Erie's 66-member group of 0-6-0 switchers, constructed by four different builders between 1904 and 1912. The Erie preferred the New York airpump to the Westinghouse model, as is evident in the photograph. [W. S. Kuba]

Engine 045, one of six normal 0-6-0's built in 1904, was converted to a tank switcher by the Erie for switching dead locomotives around the shops in Meadville, Pennsylvania. Consequently, it was one of the last steam locomotives to be scrapped. [H. N. Proctor]

A fleet of 25 beautifully maintained 4-6-0's, 950–974, built by Baldwin in 1903–1904, provided motive power for branchline local and commuter trains into Jersey City, New Jersey. As shown by the 962 and 966, they had been rebuilt with Walschaerts or Baker valve gear and piston-valve cylinders. [Both views: R. A. LeMassena]

The Erie's first 4-6-2's, built for mainline passenger trains in the 1905–1908 period, eventually superseded lighter locomotives for mainline and branch local trains radiating from Jersey City, New Jersey. There were 59 of them, Numbers 2510–2568, and after they had been rebuilt with new cylinders and valve gear, they were excellently maintained. This one was No. 2541 at Sloatsburg, New York. [R. A. LeMassena]

No. 2509 was one-of-a-kind; it had been an experimental locomotive built by American in 1910, and numbered "50,000." Its dimensions were the basis for a new group of 4-6-2's, numbered 2900–2914, erected in 1913 and 1917. [R. A. LeMassena]

A new design of 4-6-2, with smaller driving wheels, was embodied in 44 engines built during 1913–1916. These were followed by 10 more — Numbers 2744–2753 — in 1923. Then, in 1929, the Erie's shops rebuilt those last 10, giving them larger drivers and a Worthington feedwater heater. They were assigned to medium-distance medium-weight passenger trains, as exemplified by the 2752 at Croxton, New Jersey. [R. A. LeMassena]

For long-distance fast mainline passenger trains, the Erie bought 20 USRA standard heavy 4-6-2's, the only ones constructed. In 1923, 10 more arrived, embodying some improvements (feedwater heater, trailing-truck booster). And, in 1926, one "super 4-6-2," No. 2960, was delivered for service on the *Erie Limited.* However, it differed little from the previous engines, and it was the railroad's last steam passenger engine. During World War II, several of these big 4-6-2's were rebuilt with one-piece cast frames, Boxpok driver centers and 12-wheel tenders. They were then assigned to the 729-mile run between Jersey City, New Jersey, and Marion, Ohio. [R. A. LeMassena, Allan Sherry Collection]

At one time 2-8-0's, like the 1673, were the Erie's mainline freight power. A great many were rebuilt with new cylinders and valve gear for local and branchline service. Replaced by 2-8-2's or even 0-8-0's, a few were retained for transfer service between the Jersey City docks and the freight yards at Secaucus, New Jersey. [W. S. Kuba]

Of the Erie's 211 2-8-2's, produced by all three major builders from 1911 to 1923, only 20 differed from those numbered 3000–3199. Both the 3106 and 3194 had lost their small cylindrical tenders when they were modified with Elesco (No. 3106) or Worthington (No. 3194) feedwater heaters. The 3194 had received a trailing-truck booster, and the 3106 still retained its early model of Baker valve gear. Lima, Ohio, and Salamanca, New York, were the two locations for these views. [W. S. Kuba]

Erie's common switcher, found all over the system, was the 0-8-0, 16 of which were standard USRA models, Numbers 120–135, equipped with rectangular tenders, and 55 USRA duplicates, Numbers 200–254, constructed by both Baldwin and American between 1918–1930. The 200's were delivered with large 12-wheel tenders, which were exchanged for small cylindrical ones from 4-6-2's and 2-8-2's. [I. W. Saunders]

It can be said the Erie's 105 2-8-4's — received from American, Baldwin and Lima between 1927 and 1929 — saved the railroad from a total operational collapse. This was the largest group of that wheel arrangement, as well as the heaviest, 469,000 pounds for the engine and 378,000 pounds for the tender, loaded with 28 tons of coal and 21,000 gallons of water. Physically, there was little difference among them. All were equipped with trailing-truck boosters and double-guide crossheads, which were changed to single after a decade of service. The American engines had that company's standard trailing truck, but all of the others had Lima's design, which transmitted the tractive force through the truck frame. Right behind the 3305's tender was a big 4-8-4 enroute to the Santa Fe. The 3342's tender was equipped with a tender booster for some train-tonnage tests. [W. S. Kuba, H. K. Vollrath Collection]

Erie 2–10–2's came in three different models, all built between 1915 and 1919, a total of 97 locomotives. Although their cylinders were almost identical, and their driver diameters and steam pressures were alike, their boiler diameters, grate areas and trailing trucks differed considerably. The 4100–4129 possessed the biggest boilers and grate area, 104 inches and 95 square feet respectively, and the 4200–4224 (USRA heavy 2–10–2 design) had the smallest dimensions, as well as Southern valve gear. A few were given trailing-truck boosters and Elesco feedwater heaters. All of them worked as road engines and helpers in the coal-producing region of eastern Pennsylvania. [H. K. Vollrath Collection (two views), W. S. Kuba]

Toward the end of World War I, United States locomotive builders possessed 100 light 2-10-0's, which could not be delivered to Tsarist Russia's railroads. So, they were converted from five-foot gauge to standard gauge, and leased to American railroads. The Erie bought 75 of them in 1921, and assigned them to secondary lines with light rail. Three of them, Numbers 2466 and 2428 up front and No. 2492 pushing on the rear, took a railfan trip from Stroudsburg to Wilkes-Barre, Pennsylvania, in 1938. [R. A. LeMassena]

When the Lackawanna purchased the Harlem Transfer Company in 1905, that dock-switching railroad was using an 0-4-0T, No. 1, erected by Baldwin in 1898. After an oil-electric unit was acquired in 1926, the little engine was kept in the DL&W roundhouse in Hoboken, New Jersey, substituting on occasion for shop switcher No. 4. [R. A. LeMassena]

Having 100 square feet of grate area and 220 psi. steam pressure, the Lehigh & Hudson River's 2-8-0's, numbered 90–95 (built by Baldwin in 1925 and 1927), were the most powerful of their wheel arrangement. Only the Delaware & Hudson's unsuccessful experimentals surpassed their 318,000-pound weight. [R. A. LeMassena]

The Lehigh & Hudson River's eight 2-8-2's were evenly divided between the smaller 1916 design, with 100 square feet of grate area — the largest ever on a 2-8-2 — and the 1918 USRA standard design. The latter were modified by the addition of a Worthington feedwater heater and an additional airpump. [H. K. Vollrath Collection]

Acquired during World War II, the L&HR's three 4–8–2's, duplicates of the Boston & Maine's design, were among the heaviest of that wheel arrangement. Unfortunately, they were displaced by diesel-electric units after only six years of service. [H. K. Vollrath Collection]

The only Lehigh & New England locomotives built by American (1912), the seven 2-8-0's numbered 301–307, were only slightly lighter than those of the Lehigh & Hudson River. All were equipped with a booster on the rear tender truck. [H. K. Vollrath Collection]

Believe it or not, this 0-6-0 was the Lehigh & New England's newest locomotive, having been delivered by Baldwin in 1936. The railroad's biggest switcher was No. 137, an 0-8-0 having 95 square feet of grate area and a 270,000-pound weight, surpassed only by that of the Pennsylvania's engines. [H. K. Vollrath]

Needing more locomotives in 1941, the L&NE bought four 2-8-2's from the Pennsylvania, numbering them 501–504. [H. K. Vollrath Collection]

The L&NE's four 2-10-0's were dimensional twins of the enormous engines of the Western Maryland, as well as heavier than those of the Pennsylvania Railroad. Moreover, their tender boosters added 16,000 pounds to their 90,000 pounds of tractive effort, making them more potent than the USRA standard 2-8+8-2 Mallet. [H. K. Vollrath Collection]

LV 4-6-2's, 107 of which had been built between 1913 and 1924, came in two varieties, those with 77-inch drivers for passenger service, and others with 73-inch drivers for fast-freight trains. Three of the passenger engines, Numbers 2089, 2093 and 2097, and two freight engines, Numbers 2101 and 2102, were given streamlined treatment in 1939 for new passenger trains. For a short time in 1938, though, the 2101 was painted a gaudy combination of aluminum, gray, red, yellow and black. [H. K. Vollrath Collection, R. A. LeMassena]

The Lehigh Valley possessed a great many switchers, but only those numbered 3176–3210 had single cabs. All of them had been 2-8-0's, which were converted between 1919 and 1929. [H. K. Vollrath Collection]

The Lehigh Valley was the first customer for three-cylinder locomotives promoted by American in the mid-1920's. Six of them, 4-8-2's numbered 5000–5005, were assigned to passenger trains between Wilkes-Barre and Mauch Chunk, Pennsylvania. In 1939, the railroad rebuilt them into two-cylinder engines, equipping them with Boxpok drivers, two compound air compressors and huge 12-wheel tenders. Thereafter, they handled freight trains west of Wilkes-Barre. [H. K. Vollrath Collection]

At one time during the mid-1920's, half of the Lehigh Valley's locomotives were 2-8-2's, the first of which had been built in 1907; and the final 20 were the consequence of rebuilding 2-10-2's in the railroad's shops in 1928-1929, Numbers 275-294. The best performers, however, were engines in the 440-499 group, equipped with trailing-truck boosters, erected by American during 1923-1924. [Both views: H. K. Vollrath Collection]

Pulled by streamlined 4-6-2 No. 2102, the new passenger train *John Wilkes* departed Hillside Station, New Jersey, on its inaugural run in 1939. Prior to its modification, the 1916-model locomotive had been assigned to fast-freight service. [R. A. LeMassena]

Only a couple of the Eastern coal-hauling railroads utilized the 2-10-2 type; the Lehigh Valley was an exception with its fleet of 76 engines in this category, all from Baldwin in 1917–1919. Sixteen were sold to the Hocking Valley; 20 were rebuilt into 2-8-2's; and many were modified with enormous tenders equipped with boosters. Their grates had 100 square feet of grate area, more than that of the 4-8-4's. [H. K. Vollrath Collection]

Until 1939, the LV had no motive power for handling time-sensitive freight, but within five years, it had purchased 27 4-8-4's, the last five of which had 77-inch drivers for heavy passenger trains. Both Baldwin and American constructed them, a final five having been erected by American in 1943. Most of them, like the 5100, were equipped with tender boosters, but these were removed when they wore out, and trailing-truck boosters were applied instead. [R. A. LeMassena, H. K. Vollrath Collection]

A 2-4-0 was a rare locomotive indeed, but in 1939 the Morristown & Erie, in northeastern New Jersey, was still using its No. 7, constructed by American in 1905. [R. A. LeMassena]

The New York Central's little 2-4-4T's, 10 of which had been built in 1910 and 1912, were used in suburban service out of New York City. [I. W. Saunders]

More powerful than the New York Central's other 4-8-4's, and slightly smaller and lighter than the Norfolk & Western's engines, No. 6000 equalled the latter's drawbar-horsepower — 5,300 — an unsurpassed figure. This scene shows it departing La Salle Street Station in Chicago in 1952. [R. A. LeMassena]

The New York Central System's oldest-and-smallest 4-6-0's, built between 1899 and 1902 for two branches terminating at Kingston, New York, remained on those lines after the original companies had been absorbed by the NYC. The last ones of that wheel arrangement, Numbers 846–876 were constructed in 1908 for passenger service on the NYC's major branches and secondary lines. [Both views: C. W. Burns Collection]

Because the railroad's mainline was nearly level, the predominant passenger motive power was the 4-6-2, 291 of which were acquired between 1904 and 1927. No. 4803, one of five delivered in 1925, was among the first of the "modern" engines equipped with a front-end throttle and trailing-truck booster. Note that its smokebox bears a Lima builder's plate, although the engine was constructed by American. The 4925–4940 were the last 4-6-2's, and despite their trailing-truck boosters and feedwater heaters, they weighed slightly less than the Pennsylvania's 4-6-2's. [C. W. Burns, H. K. Vollrath Collection]

After diesel-electric units had replaced steam power on passenger trains, the New York Central's 4-6-4's were utilized on mail trains. Their long consists — 20 to 30 cars — usually required a pair of 4-6-4's to maintain the high speeds of 80 to 100 mph. between stops. This pair was the 5418 and 5444, shown departing Chicago with the *Fast Mail* in 1952. [R. A. LeMassena]

By the mid-1920's, passenger-train weights were straining the abilities of the NYC's heaviest 4-6-2's; so, in 1927, the first 4-6-4 was received from American. Its increased steam pressure and larger grate area enabled it to develop 30 percent more drawbar-horsepower. As the design was improved in 255 engines ordered over a decade, the pressure was increased to 275 psi., and the power developed was nearly 4,000 drawbar-horsepower. Like the 5438, the engines were delivered with 12-wheel tenders, but 50 of the later ones, like Numbers 5444 and 5443, accelerating the *Fast Mail* out of Chicago in 1952, were equipped with 4-10 tenders, holding 18,000 gallons of water and 46 tons of coal, which weighed 420,000 pounds, more than the engine's 360,000 pounds. The final 10 locomotives, 5445–5454, were streamlined. [R. A. LeMassena, C. W. Burns, H. K. Vollrath Collection]

NYC trackage in West Virginia was known originally as the Kanawaha & Michigan Railroad, and it owned three 2-8-2 tank engines, which had been built just after Brooks had become part of the American Locomotive Company. Numbers 655 and 656 still bore the round Brooks plate when they were delivered in 1902; the 657 did not arrive until 1907. It appears that they were used on short, sharply curved branches to coal mines where engines could not be turned. [H. K. Vollrath Collection]

In 1916, Lima built 50 2-8-2's for the NYC; a decade later, they were rebuilt with front-end throttles, Elesco feedwater heaters and booster-equipped trailing trucks. In their declining years — the 1950's — they lost their boosters and feedwater heaters, and they were assigned to local freight service on secondary lines. The 2086 and 2394 were the ultimate 2-8-2 on the system; erected by American in 1924, they were among the last ones purchased. [C. W. Burns and R. A. LeMassena]

There were 544 4-8-2's constructed for the NYC between 1916 and 1943, 175 of which were delivered in 1929 by American, Numbers 2800–2974. They were the system's standard freight hauler, and they were remarkably close to the Pennsylvania's 4-8-2's in their basic dimensions. After a lapse of 10 years, American produced another 50, during 1940–1942, and Lima added a final 65 during 1940–1943. These later engines were somewhat heavier, weighing 400,000 pounds, with tenders adding 380,000 pounds, loaded with 15,000 gallons of water and 42 tons of coal. [C. W. Burns, H. K. Vollrath Collection]

Even though the 4-6-4's and 4-8-2's had performed magnificently during World War II, it became evident that neither locomotive would be capable of handling trains of the higher speeds expected afterward. The NYC designed a dual-purpose 4-8-4, the first one, No. 6000, having been delivered in 1945. Having 75-inch drivers, 100 square feet of grate area and 275 psi. steam pressure, it equalled the power output of the most powerful existing 4-8-4 — Norfolk & Western's — 5,300 drawbar-horsepower. It was followed by 25 more later in the year, and by a final one, equipped with poppet valves, No. 5500, in mid-1946. Initially, they replaced 4-8-2's on passenger trains; then, only a few years later, they were assigned to mail and freight trains, the victims of "diesel displacement." All of them were sold for scrap in the fall of 1955. [C. W. Jernstrom, unknown, E. L. May]

There were almost 800 0-8-0's working on the NYC, about twice as many as the much older 0-6-0 type. A large proportion were built by Lima to USRA-standard plans, like No. 7657, which was erected in 1921. Others like it were built between 1913 and 1937. Prior to the formation of the New York Central System, the individual railroads had purchased a few 0-10-0's to shove cars over the hump in classification yards. All were built about 1910, some of them in Canada, and by 1945, they had been scrapped. [C. W. Burns, C. W. Burns Collection]

The NYC's only 0-6+6-0 was purchased in 1913 to push passenger trains up the short westward grade from Albany, New York. The introduction of heavier 4-6-2's with trailing-truck boosters enabled 0-8-0's to perform the helper work more satisfactorily. [American Locomotive Company]

Long branches extending from ports on the Great Lakes into the coal regions of Pennsylvania and West Virginia required the NYC to add 60 2-6+6-2's to its roster between 1911 and 1921. Heavy 2-8-2's and 4-8-2's displaced many of them, though some were still active in 1950. [C. W. Burns]

There were nine of these ponderous 0-8+8-0 Mallets on the NYC System, all constructed between 1914 and 1921 for pushing cars over the hump in classification yards. All of them managed to survive through World War II. [J. R. Williamson Collection]

The New York, Ontario & Western owned nothing larger than a 4-6-0 for passenger service until 1922–1923, when it purchased 10 4-8-2's, Numbers 401–410, which could also replace ancient 2-8-0's on freight trains. A second group ordered in 1929, Numbers 451–460, acquired specifically for freight service, was constructed to plans for the contemporary New York Central 4-8-2's. The 453 was accelerating westward in this view, passing through Campbell Hall, New York, with a train which had come off the NYNH&H at Maybrook, New York. [R. A. LeMassena]

The NYO&W was a pioneer in the use of 2-10-2's in the northeastern U.S.A., having purchased 12 such engines in 1915. They were characterized by their large boilers, tiny drivers and general inability to haul coal over the Scranton (Pennsylvania) Branch much faster than a snail's pace. [H. K. Vollrath Collection]

Owned by the New York Central and Canadian Pacific, the Toronto, Hamilton & Buffalo was influenced by those railroads in the character of its motive power. Its two 4-6-4's, Numbers 501 and 502, had been originally NYC 5311 and 5313. Canada's only 2-8-4's were TH&B 201 and 202, constructed in American's Montreal Works in 1928 — using the basic plans of the Boston & Albany engines, whose 1930 version was almost an exact copy. [H. K. Vollrath Collection]

Unlike Western railroads, the Eastern lines preferred to group the helper locomotives at the rear of heavy freight trains. In this dramatic scene, a pair of B&O 0–8+8–0 Mallets were shoving hard against the caboose, whose all-steel construction had been designed to withstand the 210,000-pound tractive effort. [H. W. Pontin]

# Chapter III

**COMMONWEALTH OF PENNSYLVANIA**
*Alan Wood Steel*
*Baltimore & Ohio*
*Monongahela*
*Montour*
*Pennsylvania*
*Pennsylvania Power & Light*
*Pittsburgh & Lake Erie*
*Pittsburgh & West Virginia*
*Upper Merion & Plymouth*
*Western Maryland*

Eastern and western Pennsylvania were different territories. The east was characterized by anthracite (hard) coal extraction, the west by bituminous (soft). East of Harrisburg the Pennsylvania Railroad was electrified; west of that city, steam power prevailed. Steel-making was an important business in both areas, but much more so in the west than in the east. Naturally, the mighty Pennsylvania Railroad dominated the western part of the state, though it shared its quasi-monopoly with elements of the New York Central System (Pittsburgh & Lake Erie) and the Baltimore & Ohio (Western Maryland). Some railroads hauled only a single commodity: iron ore on the Bessemer & Lake Erie; coal on the Monongahela and the Montour railroads. The Pittsburgh & West Virginia not only hauled coal, but it handled considerable miscellaneous freight because its track was located around the congested Pittsburgh area. And several steel mills, because of their great expanse, owned and operated their own railroads.

By any standard, motive power was big, heavy and powerful, though passenger trains were pulled by 4-6-2's, often double-headed. The P&LE, Monongahela, Montour and the Pittsburgh & West Virginia used 2-8-2's; the PRR employed great fleets of 2-10-0's, 2-10-4's and 4-8-2's. The P&WV had a few 2-6+6-4 Mallets, while the Western Maryland operated 4-6+6-4's and 2-8+8-2's, which were assisted by huge 2-10-0's. The B&O's roster was most remarkable: heavy 2-10-2's, 4-8-2's (new, rebuilt and second-hand) and an amazing collection of Mallets in eight different wheel arrangements, with both single- and compound-expansion cylinders. Some of them were new; others had been acquired from other railroads; and the B&O's shops modified a great many in various ways. By the mid-1950's, steam power was almost extinct; the PRR's last steam operations came in late 1957, but the B&O ran some steam engines until mid-1958.

One of the Heisler's last steam-storage locomotives was this unique articulated, No. 1, constructed for the Alan Wood Steel Company in 1940. Mounted on two geared trucks, its frame supported two horizontal cylinders, which drove a transverse shaft connected to the usual longitudinal shaft. [Heisler Locomotive Works]

Baldwin produced four 0-4-0T engines in 1912, specifically for switching on the streets of Baltimore, Maryland. Two of them, the 96 and 99, were provided with slope-back tenders in 1926 to increase their operating range. [I. W. Saunders]

Twenty chunky 2-6-0's were produced by Baldwin and Lima in 1911 and 1917. All of them were assigned to the B&O Chicago Terminal Company for industrial switching duty. Equipped with Baker valve gear and rectangular tenders, the Lima engines were more modern than the earlier locomotives. [C. W. Burns]

Because the bridges on the line along the Ohio River, from Parkersburg to Kenova, West Virginia, could support only light locomotives, the B&O retained several 1908-model 4-6-0's for service there. Double-headed, they hauled freight and heavy passenger trains until 1947. [C. W. Burns]

Two 4-6-2's, Numbers 5236 and 5231, were not needed to haul a train of only six cars on the level track across northern Indiana in 1944. Most likely, one of them was needed in Chicago for a troop train. [R. A. LeMassena]

The B&O's biggest 4-6-2's were those numbered 5300–5319, built in 1927. Some of them were rebuilt in the B&O's shops during 1944–1945 with cast-steel frames and integral cylinders. Worthington feedwater heaters and roller bearings were installed, and a few were provided with large tenders having six-wheel trucks. [C. W. Burns Collection]

All of the railroad's own 0–8–0 switchers, like the 629, assigned to the B&OCT Company, were modified 2–8–0's, having quite large drivers (62 inches) for such locomotives. [C. W. Burns]

One group of 2-8-0's, delivered during 1902–1904, when the B&O was controlled by the Pennsylvania Railroad, was built to PRR plans, as is shown in this photograph of the 2256, with a Belpaire firebox and new cylinders and valve gear. [C. W. Burns]

The B&O operated four 4-6-4's, all constructed in its own shops during 1933–1936, and all having water-tube fireboxes and 350 psi. steam pressure. The 5047 had been a 4-6-2 with 74-inch drivers; the 5340, with 84-inch drivers, was entirely new, as were the 5350 and 5360, which had 80-inch drivers. Initially, No. 5360 was equipped with rotary-cam valve gear, which was removed after a year or so. They were assigned initially to the mountainous mainline between Cumberland, Maryland, and New Castle, Pennsylvania, and performed well on heavy passenger trains until their displacement by diesel-electric units about 1950. [H. K. Vollrath Collection]

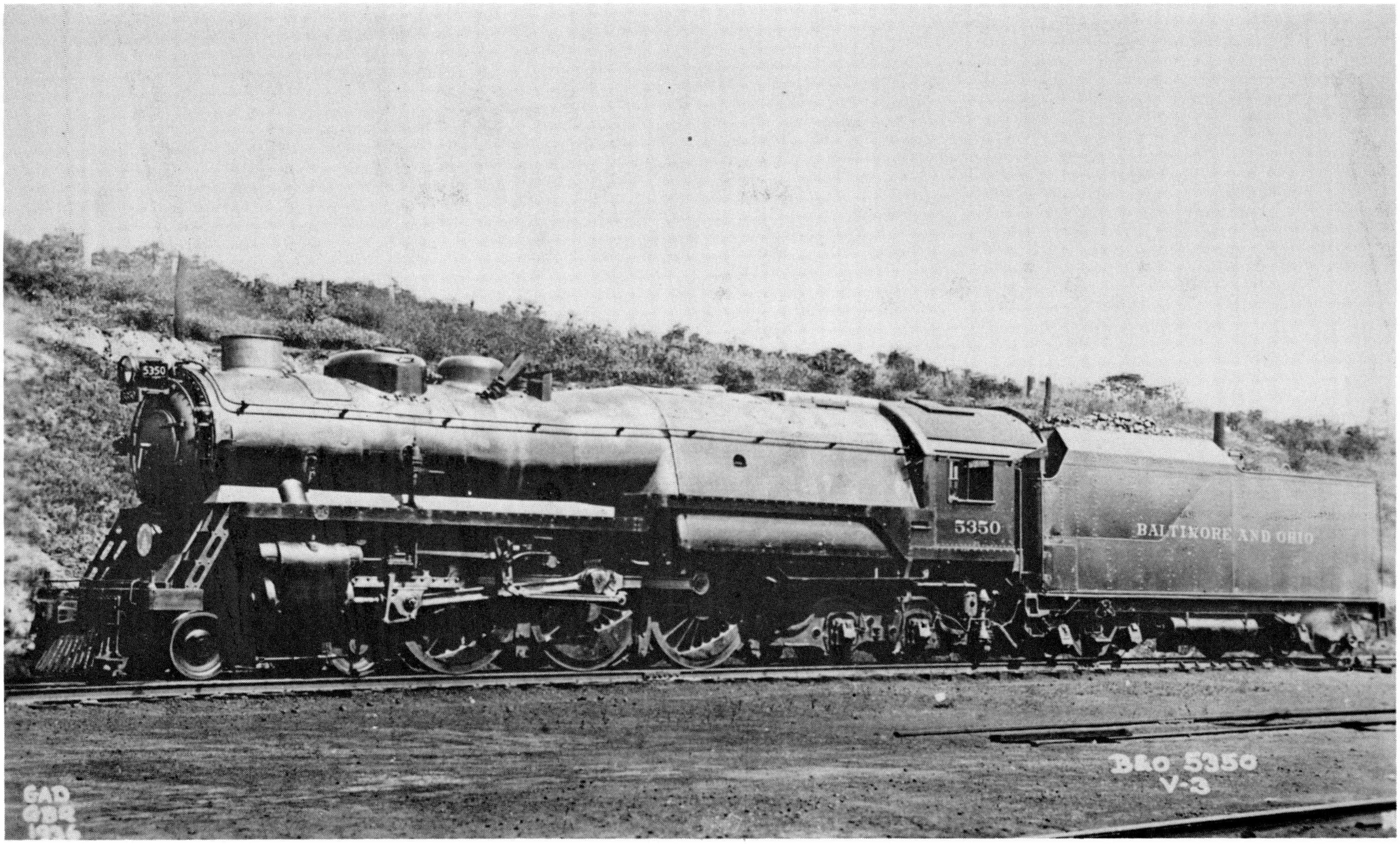
5350
BALTIMORE AND OHIO
B&O 5350
V-3

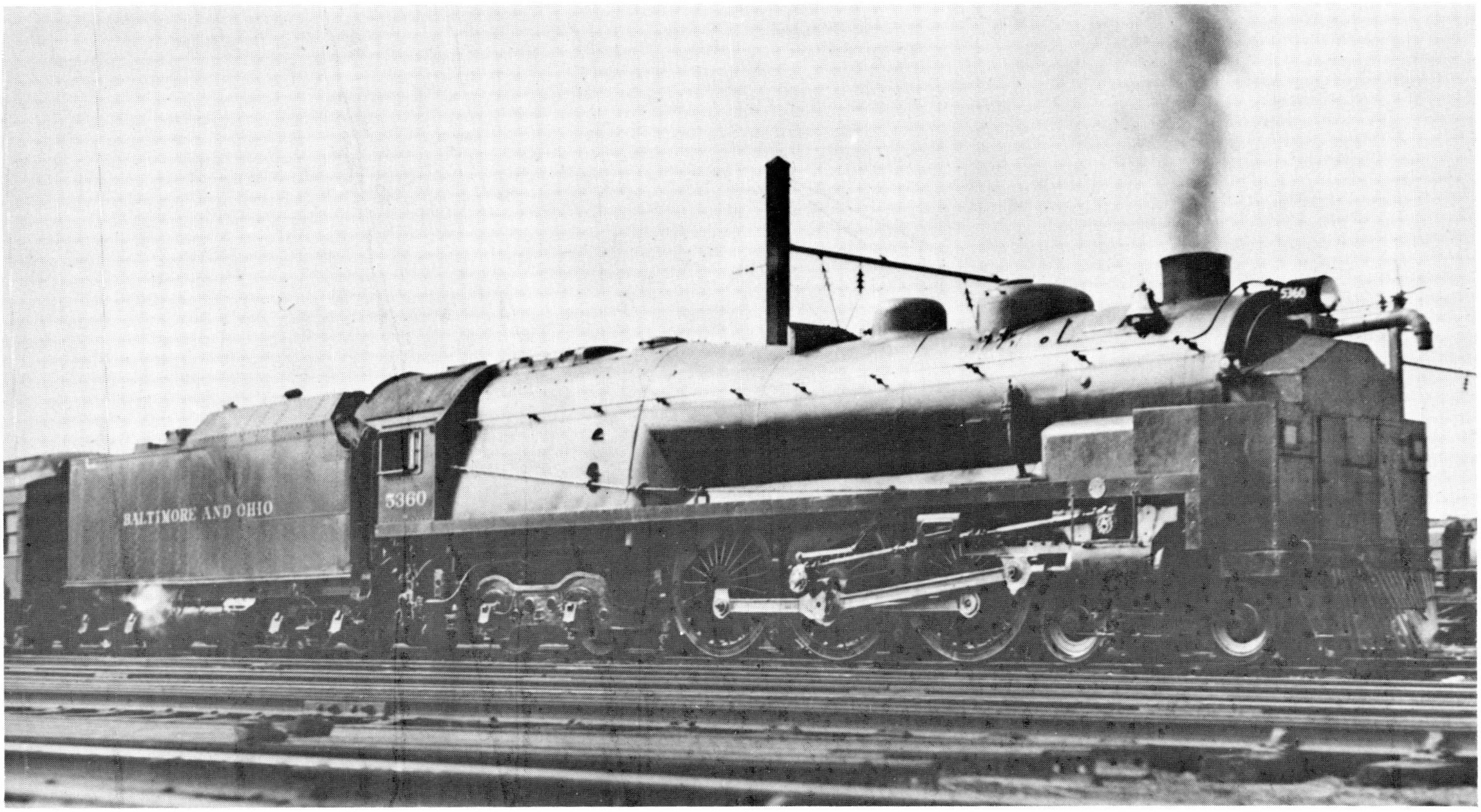
BALTIMORE AND OHIO
5360

When the B&O acquired the Chicago Terminal Transfer Railroad in 1910, it inherited four 2-8-2's, the first engines of that wheel arrangement, constructed by Brooks in 1893. It is possible that these locomotives caused the B&O to send two 2-8-0's to Baldwin in 1911 for rebuilding as its own first 2-8-2's. [H. K. Vollrath Collection]

No. 4319 was the 1913 version of the 2-8-2, whose 500+ members were produced between 1911 and 1922. Variations embraced water-tube fireboxes, 70-inch drivers and enormous cylindrical tenders. A 2-8-2, No. 4434, was the last steam locomotive operated, and one has been preserved, No. 4500. [C. W. Burns]

Between 1942 and 1948, the B&O's shops erected 40 4-8-2's, using (lengthened) boilers from 4-6-2's and 2-8-2's, supported by new one-piece cast frames. They were the last 4-8-2's constructed in the U.S.A. Seven of them were given 23-ton/22,000-gallon cylindrical tenders, instead of the 26-ton/15,000-gallon rectangular type. [Both views: C. W. Burns]

Fifteen years after the first 4-8-2 had been erected, the B&O produced its first such engines, Numbers 5500 and 5501, by placing a 2-10-2 boiler on a new 4-8-2 chassis. They were followed by a similar pair, new from Baldwin in 1930. [H. K. Vollrath Collection]

No. 5662 was one of 13 very heavy 4-8-2's purchased from the Boston & Maine in 1947. They weighed 418,000 pounds and were numbered 5650–5662. [C. W. Burns]

When the railroad built its first two 4-8-2's, using boilers from 2-10-2's, it had two surplus chassis, to which new boilers were added, thus creating a pair of 0-10-0's for hump-yard service. They bore numbers 950 and 951. [I. W. Saunders]

Among the locomotives acquired with the Buffalo, Rochester & Pittsburgh Railroad in 1932 were six 1907-vintage ugly 2-10-0's, which the B&O renumbered 6501–6506. Having tiny driving wheels — only 52 inches — they were useful only for freight yard switching. [C. W. Burns Collection]

Among the B&O's unique locomotives was the first rigid-frame 4-4 = 4-4, No. 5600, constructed in the railroad's shops in 1937. It had a water-tube firebox and 350 psi. pressure. The rear engine ran backwards, having its cylinders placed beneath the front of the firebox, requiring an unusual valve-gear configuration. [D. A. Somerville Collection]

Baldwin and Lima delivered 125 huge 2-10-2's between 1923 and 1926, numbered 6100–6224. The last groups weighed 437,000 pounds, only 3,000 pounds less than the heaviest ones — Reading's 3000–3020. Used in freight service on the two mainlines west of Cumberland, Maryland, they ended their days as transfer power with small eight-wheel tenders, like the 621 (ex-6172) in 1955. [C. W. Burns]

America's first Mallet was this 0-6+6-0, which used saturated steam and weighed 325,000 pounds, just half the weight of the B&O's big 2-8+8-4's constructed in 1944, 40 years later. [D. A. Somerville Collection]

The B&O's only new 2-6+6-2's were a pair of single-expansion locomotives delivered in 1930. Intended for fast-freight service, they were disappointments, developing little more than 3,500 drawbar-horsepower. After several years of service east of Chicago, they worked as helpers out of Cumberland, Maryland. [H. K. Vollrath Collection]

Through its Buffalo, Rochester & Pittsburgh subsidiary, the Baltimore & Ohio owned 55 compound-expansion 2-6+6-2's, 30 of which were provided with Southern valve gear, the only such application to that wheel arrangement. They were renumbered 7500–7554 in 1931, but they remained in service on BR&P trackage. [C. W. Jernstrom]

Because the Seaboard Air Line Railroad was converting to diesel-electric motive power quite early, the Baltimore & Ohio was able to buy its 10 single-expansion 2-6+6-4's in 1947, numbering them 7700–7709. They were used in fast freight service between Brunswick and Cumberland, Maryland, until their second displacement by internal-combustion motive power in 1953. [C. W. Burns Collection]

Seven years elapsed between the arrival of the first Mallet and the delivery of ten ponderous 0-8+8-0's, which were soon followed by 20 more. The 7046 was among the last ones received in 1913, and it worked as a helper on the mountainous mainlines for more than 35 years. [C. W. Jernstrom]

The sharply curved trackage on the railroad's mountain grades caused excessive flange wear on the forward drivers; so, over a period of 30 years, leading trucks were added to the 0-8+8-0's, like No. 7038. [C. W. Burns Collection]

109

Leading a long consist of empty coal cars, No. 7170 was drifting slowly down the 2.2-percent grade westbound from Altamont. Upgrade coal trains used the right-hand track, while merchandise and passenger trains occupied the center rails. [B. F. Cutler]

Engine 7154, a single-expansion 2–8+8–0, was arriving at M&K Junction, after descending the two-percent grade from the west. Two rear-end helpers were added here for the even steeper climb to Altamont, Maryland. [B. F. Cutler]

Numbers 7300–7315 possessed an adventurous career. After working only five years on the Seaboard Air Line, these Mallets were purchased by the B&O, and almost immediately lost their trailing trucks. Four years later, in 1927, they were rebuilt to single-expansion, and were provided with enormous cylindrical tenders. Despite their undersize grate area, oversize drivers and Southern valve gear, most of them remained in service until the mid-1950's. [C. W. Jernstrom]

The ex-BR&P 2–8+8–2's, renumbered to 7316–7324, possessed low-pressure cylinders 44 inches in diameter, three inches larger than anything else on the B&O. These monsters, with 57-inch drivers and a 112-inch boiler, remained on the BR&P until they were displaced by B&O 2–8+8–0's. [Howard Davis]

Between 1925 and 1930, the B&O's shops rebuilt all but two of its newest 2-8+8-0's from compound- to single-expansion, making them suitable for line-haul service. For some forgotten reason, the 7145–7170 group was built with Baker valve gear on the forward engine and Walschaerts on the rear. [Howard Davis]

Assisted by a pair of Mallet helpers pushing at the rear of this coal train, 2-8+8-4 7601 blasts up the 2.2-percent grade eastward toward Altamont. The B&O owned 30 of these modern monsters, the last ones of the wheel arrangement to have been constructed. [H. W. Pontin]

Delivered from Baldwin during 1944—1945, the 30 single-expansion 2-8+8-4's were remarkable locomotives. Only 15 feet high and weighing only 60,000 pounds on driving axles, their 64-inch drivers and full roller-bearing installation enabled them to handle passenger trains at 70 mile-per-hour speeds. They worked initially between Cumberland, Maryland, and Grafton, West Virginia, then completed their careers on the branches to coal docks on Lake Erie. [C. W. Burns]

The 7212 may have been unique. It was never converted to single-expansion; it was equipped with Baker and Walschaerts valve gear; and its smokebox door was most unusual. [C. W. Burns Collection]

In the far southwestern corner of Pennsylvania the Monongahela operated a one-car passenger train between Brownsville, Pennsylvania, and Fairmont, West Virginia. Its only passenger locomotive, an elderly 4-4-2 from the Pennsylvania Railroad, indicated one of the railroad's three owners. [C. W. Burns]

Most of the Monongahela's 52 locomotives were 2–8–2's. No. 172 was a USRA standard 2–8–2, which had been given a trailing-truck booster. It was waiting at Brownsville for a train of empties being returned to the mines. [C. W. Burns]

It was logical that Monongahela 2-8-0's resembled those of the Baltimore & Ohio; the B&O owned one-third of the 170-mile railroad. [C. W. Burns]

No. 200's portrait was made at Brownsville in 1952, the last year of all-steam operations. This had been a P&LE engine; the railroad's last new power having been Baldwin 2-8-2's, numbered 180–185, delivered in 1927. [C. W. Burns]

Both the 188 and 191 show evidence of Pittsburgh & Lake Erie ancestry because the P&LE was the third owner of the Monongahela. Note how the tender's water- and-coal capacities have been increased. [C. W. Burns]

Owned by a coal company since 1917, the Montour Railroad was acquired by the Pennsylvania and the Pittsburgh & Lake Erie railroads in 1947. Its 51-mile mainline, connecting the P&LE at Coraopolis with the Pittsburgh & West Virginia at Mifflin, Pennsylvania, formed a semicircle in the hilly territory west of Pittsburgh. Its original locomotives were 2-8-2's, numbered 20–35. [H. K. Vollrath Collection]

Subsequent locomotive acquisitions were Numbers 40 and 41 from the New York Central; Numbers 42–45, ex-Virginian Numbers 427, 438, 456 and 461; and Numbers 50–52, ex-DL&W Numbers 2101, 2138 and 2102. [Railroad Museum of Pennsylvania (PHMC); three photos H. K. Vollrath Collection]

121

The Pennsylvania Railroad, known for the fast schedules of its passenger trains, built the first of 601 4-4-2's in 1899, and subsequently erected No. 3151 in 1906. It was among the first PRR locomotives to have Walschaerts valve gear, and they had 80-inch drivers, like those on the 4-4-0's. In 1936, just out of the shops after some cosmetic modifications, the engine was handling branchline trains out of Harrisburg, Pennsylvania. The ultimate 4-4-2, represented by the 1477 on a local train at Farmington, New Jersey, had an outside-bearing trailing truck. The railroad built 82 of them in 1912 and 1914, and many of them were still running in the early 1950's [C. W. Burns Collection, R. A. LeMassena]

Although the Pennsylvania used a hundred or so 4-6-0's, it abandoned that wheel arrangement in 1901 in favor of powerful-and-fast 4-4-2's. Then, in 1923 and 1929, the PRR built 121 of them specifically for commuter service and branch-line work. Excepting one Southern Pacific engine, they were the heaviest 4-6-0's, and No. 50, assigned to the Long Island Railroad, was the last of that type constructed. All of them were operated until 1949, and all of them — excepting No. 5741, which has been preserved — had been scrapped by 1954. [C. W. Burns]

The last — and most modern — group of 0-4-0's consisted of 47 engines built in the PRR's shops during 1916–1917 and in 1924, all like the 891. They were used around Philadelphia for industrial and dock switching, where they were so indispensable that none were retired until 1948. [H. K. Vollrath Collection]

Whereas other large railroads relied on the common 0–8–0 switcher, the PRR used only 90, all built in its own shops during 1925 and 1927. The heaviest of that wheel arrangement, they possessed the same axle load as the 2–10–4's, 70,000 pounds. They worked in major freight yards, where the track could support them, and they even handled transfer runs between yards. All of them were set aside between 1948 and 1952. [C. W. Burns]

The most common switcher on the Pennsylvania's system was the familiar 0-6-0 with Belpaire firebox, many of which were erected by the railroad as late as 1926. No. 218 was an early model — 1907 vintage. The 1913 group was unusual because they were just about the only PRR engines which had a radial-stay firebox. No. 9990 was one of 30 USRA standard engines, and the last one to be retired, in 1952. Switcher No. 5244 was the last steam locomotive operated by the railroad — in July of 1959 — one and one-half years after the "official" end of steam operations. [Two upper views: C. W. Burns Collection, lower view: C. W. Burns]

In the same year that the Pennsylvania built its last 4-4-2, in 1914, it produced the first of 425 4-6-2's, all alike, 75 of which were constructed by Baldwin in 1927, Numbers 5400-5474. It would not be inaccurate to say that they were "stretched" 4-4-2's, because they had the same driver diameter and essentially identical boiler diameters. During World War II, double-heading was very common, as indicated by the 5352 and 5451, with the *Admiral* at Chicago. There were many mechanical variations: No. 3768 was streamlined and had a 12-wheel tender; the 5399 was rebuilt with Franklin oscillating-cam poppet-valves; No. 3747 received Franklin rotary-cam poppet valves. They were still hauling passenger trains in local service until the end of steam in 1957, and two of them have been preserved, one operational and one exhibited. [Upper view: R. A. LeMassena; the three other views: H. K. Vollrath Collection]

The 4644 was one of 475 2-10-0's constructed by Baldwin in 1923 for the Pennsylvania. It was modified in 1943, receiving a feedwater heater and superheater. Its original 4-4 tender was replaced with a larger 6-6 model, which itself was replaced with one of the monstrous 8-8 tenders whose loaded weight was greater than the engine. [R. R. Malinoski]

The 2-8-2 was the natural successor to the 2-8-0, and the PRR had 579 of them, built by Lima, Baldwin and its own shops from 1914 through 1919. They utilized the same boiler as the 4-6-2's, but one was given a water-tube firebox. Their 62-inch drivers were the same as those on 2-8-0's, and trailing-truck boosters were applied to a few of them. Some were sold to other railroads during World War II; AT&SF No. 882 and Detroit, Toledo & Ironton No. 317 among them. [C. W. Burns; two photos: H. K. Vollrath Collection]

In 1924, the PRR's roster included 3,335 2-8-0's, 44 percent of the railroad's entire steam roster. They were built from 1875 until 1915 by Baldwin, American and the PRR's own shops. The 1932 had come from Baldwin in 1911, while the 9783 came from Baldwin in 1915. They were retired in 1949 and 1951, but a great many were still running in the late 1950's. [C. W. Burns Collection, C. W. Burns]

Until the 4-8-2 was developed, the Pennsylvania did not have a locomotive for fast freight service. That need was met in 1923 by a homemade model which joined a modified 2-10-0 boiler, with a 98-inch combustion chamber, to a chassis accommodating 72-inch drivers. However, two years of testing were needed to convince officials of its abilities. Then, 200 more were built by Baldwin and Lima in 1926, and in 1930, the railroad's shops joined them in constructing 100 more. Initially, 30 were assigned to passenger service between Harrisburg, Pennsylvania, and Columbus, Ohio, using 4-4 tenders. In time they were replaced with the standard 6-6 tenders, and many of these were superseded by 8-8 tenders, which, when loaded with 24,000 gallons of water and 25 tons of coal, weighed 26,000 pounds more than the engine's 382,000 pounds. The 6967, a Baldwin engine, was photographed at Huntingdon, Pennsylvania. [R. A. LeMassena]

The movement of coal during World War I was the catalyst for the development of the Pennsylvania's 2-10-0, another variation of the 2-8-0 chassis, with 62-inch drivers. The boiler, though enlarged, retained the same grate area, but its steam pressure was much higher, 250 psi. The first one emerged from Altoona's shops in 1916, soon followed by 122 more. Baldwin produced the next 475, completing in 1923 the largest single locomotive order. Eventually, all of them were superheated and equipped with Worthington feedwater heaters and stokers. Early tenders rode on four-wheel trucks; then came six-wheel trucks, and finally, 21,000-gallon, 30-ton tenders with eight-wheel trucks. As both road engine and helper, they were operated all over Pennsylvania and eastern Ohio until the end of steam in 1957. No. 4483 has been preserved. [H. K. Vollrath Collection]

Because of its east-end electrification project, the PRR had not added any new freight locomotives since 1930, but the immense traffic generated by World War II necessitated the immediate construction of 125 2-10-4's from plans of the outstanding Chesapeake & Ohio engines. An inch was added to the driver diameter (70 inches); steam pressure was increased to 270 psi.; and the weight went to 578,000 pounds, making them the heaviest ones ever built. Almost overnight, they dominated the mainlines west of Altoona, Pennsylvania. Diesel-electric units displaced all of them in 1957. No. 6166 was photographed at Columbus; No. 6159 at Canton, Ohio. [R. A. LeMassena, C. W. Burns]

The Pennsylvania's 2-10-2's could be considered a more powerful 2-8-2 or a speedier 2-10-0. It possessed the latter's cylinders, the former's trailing truck, and the common driver size. The boiler was enlarged to 99 inches in diameter, and the grate area to 80 square feet. Sixty were received from American and Baldwin during 1919, and they went to work hauling coal and iron ore between Lake Erie ports and the mines and steel mills in eastern Ohio and western Pennsylvania. They were joined by 130 more of USRA standard design from the same builders. In 1923, the railroad's shops modified them with Walschaerts valve gear, Belpaire firebox and standard front end. The 7242 was photographed at Canton, Ohio, the 7910 at Columbus. [Both views: C. W. Burns]

In its attempt to avoid the very successful 4-8-4 wheel arrangement, the Pennsylvania, collaborating with American, Baldwin and Lima designers, assembled a monstrous duplex 6-4 = 4-6 in 1939. Its boiler carried 300 psi. pressure, and its drivers were 84 inches in diameter. Few Mallets had larger grate areas — 132 square feet — or greater weight — 608,000 pounds — and no other locomotive came close to its 124-foot total wheelbase. Its 8-8 tender, loaded with 24,000 gallons of water and 27 tons of coal, weighed 452,000 pounds. It was so big that it could be operated only between Crestline, Ohio, and Chicago. It was shown at the New York World's Fair in 1939, but a decade later, it was scrapped. [H. K. Vollrath Collection]

The first two 4-4 = 4-4's, one with a trailing-truck booster, delivered by Baldwin in 1942, were an outgrowth of the much-too-big 6-4 = 4-6. Wartime restrictions prevented further construction, yet the Pennsylvania tested a much superior Norfolk & Western 4-8-4 in 1944. It was surprising then, that the PRR built 25 more (the last steam locomotives erected by the railroad), and obtained another 25 from Baldwin in 1946, all with poppet valves, but without boosters to help these slippery engines during starting. In an attempt to correct traction problems, the 5500 was rebuilt with rotary-can poppet valves, and the 5547 was rebuilt with Walschaerts valve gear, all to no avail. Most of them were retired in 1952 and 1953, but a few lingered until 1956. [C. W. Burns, H. K. Vollrath Collection, I. W. Saunders]

135

In an attempt to develop a faster-and-more-powerful freight locomotive, the PRR designed a four-cylinder 4-6 = 4-4 duplex with 77-inch drivers, but with only 98 square feet of grate area. Its boiler carried 300 psi. steam pressure, and a booster was installed on the trailing truck. Erected in 1942, its performance was inadequate to justify duplication, and it was retired in 1952. [H. K. Vollrath Collection]

Despite the success of existing six-axle articulateds capable of developing 6,000-8,000 drawbar-horsepower, the Pennsylvania's designers clung to the five-axle divided-drive concept in a final attempt to move more tonnage at faster speeds with lower cost. And they succeeded — but too late to resist conversion to internal-combustion motive power. They placed an enormous boiler, with a 106-inch maximum diameter, 122 square feet of grate area and 300 psi. steam pressure, on a 4-4 = 6-4 four-cylinder chassis. Its 124-inch combustion chamber set a new record, and the engine's weight, 725,000 pounds, equalled that of the Chesapeake & Ohio's 2-6+6-6. Although it produced 7,000 horsepower at the rails, erratic power surges between front and rear cylinders led to their early retirement in 1953–1955, merely a decade after their birth in the Altoona shops. [C. W. Burns]

The Pennsylvania experimented with articulateds quite early with a 2-8+8-2, built by American in 1911; a 0-8+8-0, built by Baldwin in 1912; and a 2-8+8-0, built in the company shops in 1919. In that same year, it bought 10 Baldwin 0-8+8-0's for helper service on the hill west of Altoona. Displaced by 2-10-0's, they subsequently worked as helpers on lake port trains, and as transfer power at Columbus, Ohio, where this photograph of the 7335 was taken. All were gone by 1949. [C. W. Burns]

For the next quarter century, the railroad ignored articulateds; however, desperate for locomotives during World War II, the PRR bought six 2-8+8-2's from the Norfolk & Western, then scrapped them five years later. Only the classification lights and the number "374" in the keystone emblem indicate PRR ownership of this Mallet. [O. C. Perry]

The Pittsburgh & Lake Erie's 10 1916-model New York Central standard 4-6-2's were supplemented by 10 more in 1930, Numbers 9245–9254, from the Boston & Albany, which had received 10 new 4-6-4's. Having smaller drivers — 75 inches — and trailing-truck boosters, they were ideal engines for the P&LE's short-run passenger trains. [H. K. Vollrath Collection]

The seven 2-8-4's delivered in 1948 present an enigma. They had lower boiler pressure, smaller grate area, smaller cylinders, but greater weight than the Boston & Albany engines of 1926–1930. They were the only NYC System locomotives with vestibule-type cabs, and their elongated tenders held only 20,000 gallons of water and 22 tons of coal. Three of the original order were scrapped before they were completed in American's factory, and they were the last steam locomotives built by that company in the U.S.A. Displaced by diesel-electric units after working only five years, they were scrapped after another two years of service in Ohio. [C. W. Burns Collection]

The P&LE's enormous coal-and-ore tonnage required powerful 2-8-2's, the first of 65 arriving in 1916. Half of them had tiny drivers, only 57 inches in diameter. Twenty more — Numbers 191–211 — with 63-inch drivers, arrived in 1923–1924. All of them had been built by American. In 1945, some of the earliest ones were sold to Pemex, Mexico's national petroleum company, which later transferred them to the National Railway System. [I. W. Saunders, unknown]

Like other companies in the New York Central System, the P&LE employed monstrous 0-8+8-0 Mallets to shove cars over the humps in classification yards. Two of them, the 9090 and the 9091, were delivered in 1916. Their low-pressure cylinders were 40 inches in diameter. [C. W. Burns Collection]

Only one 0-8-0 steam-storage engine was ever built. Heisler constructed it in 1939 as Hammermill Paper Company No. 4, but it was soon resold to the Pennsylvania Power & Light Company in Hauto, in the hard-coal region of eastern Pennsylvania. Numbered 4906-D, it is displayed at the State Museum in Strasburg, Pennsylvania. [B. F. G. Kline, Jr. Collection]

Before the Pittsburgh & West Virginia constructed its extension from Pierce (south of Pittsburgh) to a connection with the Western Maryland at Connellsville, Pennsylvania, in 1930, it operated passenger trains powered by three 4-6-2's built by American in 1921 and 1924. When the P&WV discontinued passenger trains in 1931, the 4-6-2's were assigned to local freight trains. [H. K. Vollrath Collection]

The P&WV's newest 2-8-0's were Numbers 923–928, delivered in 1921. Once each day, one of them ran over Wheeling & Lake Erie trackage to Brewster, Ohio, where this photograph was taken. [C. W. Burns]

Only three of the P&WV's 2-8-2's were new, Numbers 1000–1002, delivered by Baldwin in 1918. After World War II, No. 1010 was obtained from the Chicago, Indianapolis & Louisville, and Numbers 1050–1053 came from the Central Railroad of New Jersey. [C. W. Burns and H. K. Vollrath Collection]

The Connellsville Extension established a new freight route by joining the Western Maryland and the Reading on the east to the Wheeling & Lake Erie and New York, Chicago & St. Louis on the west. Handling the new through traffic required the acquisition of seven remarkable 2-6+6-4's from Baldwin in 1934–1937. All had Belpaire fireboxes, and the first three came equipped with 6-B1 booster-powered tenders. They were operated over the segment between Connellsville and Rook Yard, west of Pittsburgh.  [C. W. Burns Collection, J. F. Humiston]

The Alan Wood Steel Company in Conshohocken, Pennsylvania, near Philadelphia, owned the Upper Merion & Plymouth Railroad, which used a pair of tiny 0-4-2 tank engines for hauling coal, ore, limestone and slag over the light and often temporary track around the mill. [H. K. Vollrath Collection]

All of the Western Maryland's 4-6-2's were built by Baldwin between 1909 and 1912. The first ones, numbered 151–160, lasted until 1943, when they were sold to the Seaboard Air Line. Numbers 201–209 were slightly larger and heavier, and they handled mainline passenger trains until 1954. [H. K. Vollrath Collection]

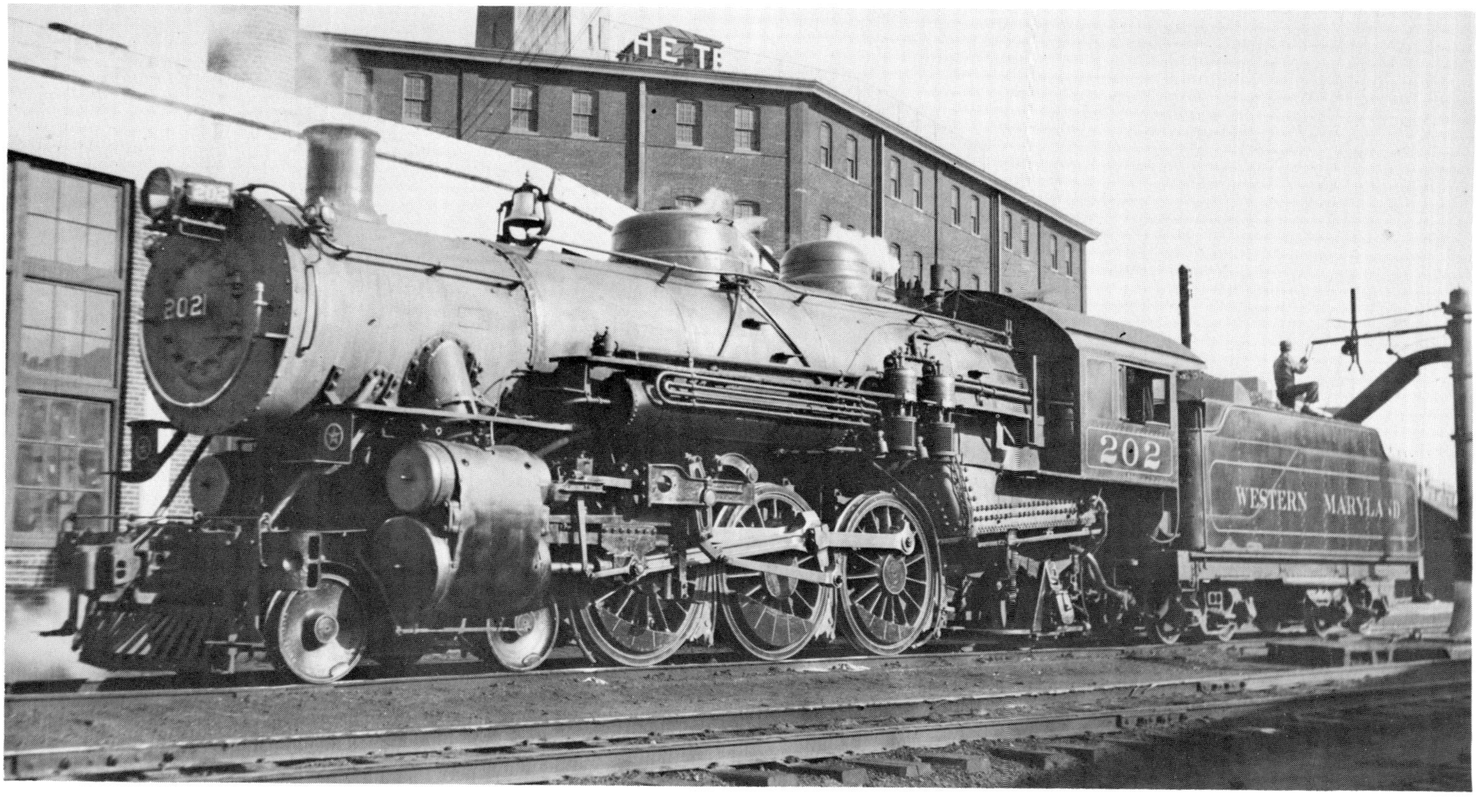

For a railroad of its size, the Western Maryland possessed an amazingly large number of 2-8-0's — more than 250 of them — and the final 50 were among the heaviest of that wheel arrangement. Numbers 801–850 came from Baldwin's factory in 1921 and 1923. They weighed 286,000 pounds, unsurpassed at that time. As many as 10 of them would be assigned to a 7,500-ton coal train on the three-percent grade eastward from Elkins, West Virginia. The 803 had been modified by the addition of a Worthington feedwater heater. [I. W. Saunders, G. C. Cory]

WM 2-10-0's came in two sizes: very small and very large. The 10 little ones, Numbers 401–410, had been built for the Tsarist Russian government, but were sold to American railroads in 1919, following the Russian Revolution. Most of them were still running in 1950. The big ones weighed 420,000 pounds, almost twice as much as the earlier "Russian Decapods" (as the little 2-10-0's were called), and they were among the heaviest of this wheel arrangement. Their loaded tenders weighed the same as the engine. Their boilers were larger than the famous Pennsylvania 2-10-0, and their grate area, 105 square feet, was 50 percent greater. Delivered in 1927, they remained in service until they were replaced by diesel-electric locomotives. They were numbered 1111–1130. [Both views: H. K. Vollrath Collection]

The WM's 12 4-8-4's, though overshadowed by the Norfolk & Western's locomotives, deserved better recognition. Their boilers, 106 inches in diameter, were four inches bigger than that of any other 4-8-4, and their grate area, cylinder size and driver diameter were just slightly smaller than those of the N&W 4-8-4. Few 4-8-4's surpassed their 507,000-pound weight. Loaded with 30 tons of coal and 22,000 gallons of water, their tenders weighed 420,000 pounds. Not only were they Baldwin's last 4-8-4's, but they were also the last new design of the 4-8-4 wheel arrangement. Delivered in 1947, they were used for only seven years on the mainlines east of Cumberland, Maryland. [I. W. Saunders]

The nine 2-6+6-2 Mallets, which the Western Maryland purchased between 1909 and 1911, used saturated steam, and all four cylinders had slide valves, old features which were never changed. In 1927, when the heavier and more powerful 2-10-0's arrived, they were converted to yard switchers by the removal of their front and rear trucks. The 952 survived until 1952, outliving all the others. [H. K. Vollrath Collection]

Lima's first Mallets, and its only 2-8+8-2's, were those built for the WM, Numbers 901–915, erected in 1915 and 1916, and Numbers 916–925, delivered in 1917 and 1918. Despite identical specifications, the two groups differed mechanically. The latter engines had piston valves for the low-pressure cylinders and the uncommon Jacobs-Shupert firebox, with a smaller grate area. Numbers 923 and 924 were equipped with a booster on the rear tender truck. [H. K. Vollrath Collection]

It was evident that the WM's locomotives could not move the increasing non-coal freight fast enough; so the railroad acquired 4-6+6-4's in 1941, all 12 from Baldwin, and the only ones built by that company other than 15 for the Denver & Rio Grande Western in 1938 and 1942. They were given the largest boilers, but not the largest fireboxes. Until their retirement in 1953, they worked between Hagerstown, Maryland, and Connellsville, Pennsylvania. Their tenders, duplicated for the later 4-8-4's, held 30 tons of coal and 22,000 gallons of water. [Top, opposite: Unknown, G. C. Cory]

In 1944, the Western Maryland bought Lima's last Shay geared locomotive, a 324,000-pound three-truck monster and one of the heaviest constructed. For nine years it worked on a short coal-mining branch, and it was subsequently presented to the Baltimore & Ohio's museum in Baltimore, Maryland. This photograph shows it enroute in 1953, when the WM terminated steam operations. The engine has since been moved to Cass, West Virginia, where it is operated on a tourist railroad. [C. W. Jernstrom]

It was NYC&StL official policy to operate its freight trains about a fast as the law allowed. In this scene at Valparaiso, Indiana, No. 730 was running so fast that its exhaust lay back above the cars, which were stirring up a cloud of roadbed dust, just like a passenger train, doing well over 60 mph. [R. A. LeMassena]

# Chapter IV

## BEYOND THE APPALACHIANS

*Akron, Canton & Youngstown*
*Alton*
*Alton & Southern*
*Belt Railway of Chicago*
*Chicago & Calumet Terminal*
*Chicago & Illinois Midland*
*Grand Trunk Western*
*Illinois Central*
*Illinois Midland*
*New York, Chicago & St. Louis*
*River Terminal*
*Wabash*
*Wheeling & Lake Erie*

West of the mountains and north of the Ohio River lay the heart of industrial America. A region of rolling hills, modest gradients and gentle curves, it was a place where passenger trains set speed records; yet, it was where the nation's most powerful steam locomotives hauled incredible tonnages of coal, and where merchandise or perishable freight regularly moved on mile-a-minute schedules. Competition among the major railroads, Pennsylvania; Baltimore & Ohio; Erie; New York Central; New York, Chicago & St. Louis; and Wabash, was ferocious, the consequence of a dense network of interlocking trackage. The Akron, Canton & Youngstown's trackage, stretching east–west across northern Ohio, provided a convenient interchange route among larger railroads. The Alton was the B&O's affiliate, connecting Chicago, St. Louis and Kansas City, and the Chicago & Calumet Terminal was the original ancestor of the B&O Chicago Terminal Railroad. The Chicago & Illinois Midland hauled coal for its owner, Commonwealth Edison of Chicago. The NYC&StL was renowned for its high-speed freight service, while its Wheeling & Lake Erie subsidiary hauled coal out of southeastern Ohio. Wabash operations extended all the way from Kansas City to Buffalo, New York, thus eliminating delays due to interline transfers at the Mississippi River. The Illinois Central's north–south mainline connected with every railroad southward from Chicago.

Most railroads hauled passenger trains with 4-6-2's, but the Wabash, NYC&StL and NYC used 4-6-4's. The IC found it necessary to utilize 4-8-2's, as did the NYC, which later assigned 4-8-4's to fast-and-heavy consists. Instead of copying these two railroads, the PRR developed a 4-4=4-4 duplex, which atained 140 mph., despite its otherwise unreliable performance. The IC, NYC&StL, Erie and W&LE hauled freight with 2-8-4's; the NYC, PRR, B&O and IC preferred 4-8-2's. The IC used 2-10-2's, as did the PRR, which also operated a fleet of 2-10-4's and duplex 4-4=6-4's. The only freight 4-8-4's were those of the Wabash and Grand Trunk Western. Only the NYC and W&LE operated Mallets, all compound-expansion 2-6+6-2's, assigned to coal service in eastern Ohio. The Norfolk & Western and Chesapeake & Ohio penetrated Ohio from the south, and they are covered in the following section.

Very few railfans saw the Akron, Canton & Youngstown's two big 0-8-0's, numbered 37 and 38, built by Lima in 1926. They were equipped with front-end throttles and over-fire air jets. [C. W. Burns]

For its line-haul freights the AC&Y relied on seven 2–8–2's delivered in pairs bearing numbers 400–405 in 1926, 1928 and 1941, and the last in 1944. Their basic design was the 1918 USRA model, but they were equipped with quite modern improvements. [C. W. Burns]

After the Baltimore & Ohio had acquired the Chicago & Alton in 1931, the railroad was renamed the Alton Railroad, and its locomotives were renumbered in the B&O numbering series. No. 5292, built by American in 1913, had been C&A No. 652, one of the last 10 built for that railroad. Note the modifications — much larger tender, Worthington feedwater heater and air after-cooler. [H. K. Vollrath Collection]

The Chicago & Alton's most modern locomotives were USRA standard light 2-8-2's delivered by American in 1919 and 1921. The 4393 (B&O series) had been C&A's No. 883 until 1931. These locomotives, though small, were the Alton's biggest freight engines. [H. K. Vollrath Collection]

The Alton inherited a pair of 1910-model 2-6+6-2's from its corporate predecessor, the Chicago & Alton, which had sold one of its three new Mallets to the Chesapeake & Ohio only a year after delivery. [H. K. Vollrath Collection]

The Alton & Southern possessed a remarkable variety of locomotives for such a small railroad. It owned one Mallet, this 2-6+6-2 acquired from the Portland & Southwestern in 1918. [H. K. Vollrath Collection]

Another of the Alton & Southern's unique locomotives was this three-cylinder 0-8-0, which — fortunately — has been preserved in the National Museum of Transport. [C. E. Winters]

This lone 0-10-0 had an aluminum boiler jacket, crushed foil insulation, aluminum main and side rods, and a tender booster. Delivered by Baldwin in 1931, it was the last of its wheel arrangement [Unknown]

The A&S used 2-8-2's for transfer service in the St. Louis area, and No. 15, built by Baldwin in 1936, was the biggest one. Like the other locomotives, it had an aluminum jacket and insulation, as well as side and main rods. This was because the railroad was owned by ALCOA (the Aluminum Company of America). [H. K. Vollrath Collection]

In 1945 the A&S bought Delaware, Lackawanna & Western heavy 2-8-2's Numbers 2143 and 2149, renumbering them 26 and 27. The A&S modified the tenders of these engines, removed the trailing-truck booster and added a compound airpump on the pilot deck. [W. C. Witbeck]

Baldwin built only 12 three-cylinder locomotives during their mid-1920's popularity — a 4-10-2 demonstrator, 10 D&RGW 4-8-2's, and this lone 0-8-0 for the Belt Railway of Chicago. The valves of its center cylinder were actuated by Joy valve gear, the only such application other than three 4-4-2's constructed in the Philadelphia & Reading's shops. [H. K. Vollrath Collection]

Practically unknown locomotives, the four 2-8-2's which Brooks built for the Chicago & Calumet Terminal in 1893, Numbers 101–104, were the first new engines of that wheel arrangement. Eventually, they became B&O Chicago Terminal Numbers 394–397, and they were not retired until 1919. [H. K. Vollrath Collection]

Tiny railroads, like the Illinois Midland, did not need anything larger than an 0-4-0 tank engine to haul its freight trains, which rarely exceeded a single car. [D. K. Peterson]

The Chicago & Illinois Midland's three 4-4-0's, built by Baldwin in 1928, were the last of that wheel arrangement. They were used on the spotlessly maintained, but little patronized, two-car local trains operated between Pekin and Springfield, Illinois [R. A. LeMassena]

No. 540 and its twin, the 541, were 0-8-0's erected by Lima in 1937. They were the last new steam locomotives acquired by the Chicago & Illinois Midland. [R. A. LeMassena]

The C&IM's 2-8-2's were derived from a variety of sources. Numbers 525 and 526 had previously been Chesapeake & Ohio Numbers 2920 and 2921 after the acquisition of the Sewell Valley Railroad in 1927. The 550–552 group had been purchased new from Lima in 1928 and 1931. The heaviest ones, ex-Delaware, Lackawanna & Western Numbers 2120 and 2137, were renumbered 560 and 561 by the C&IM. [H. K. Vollrath Collection]

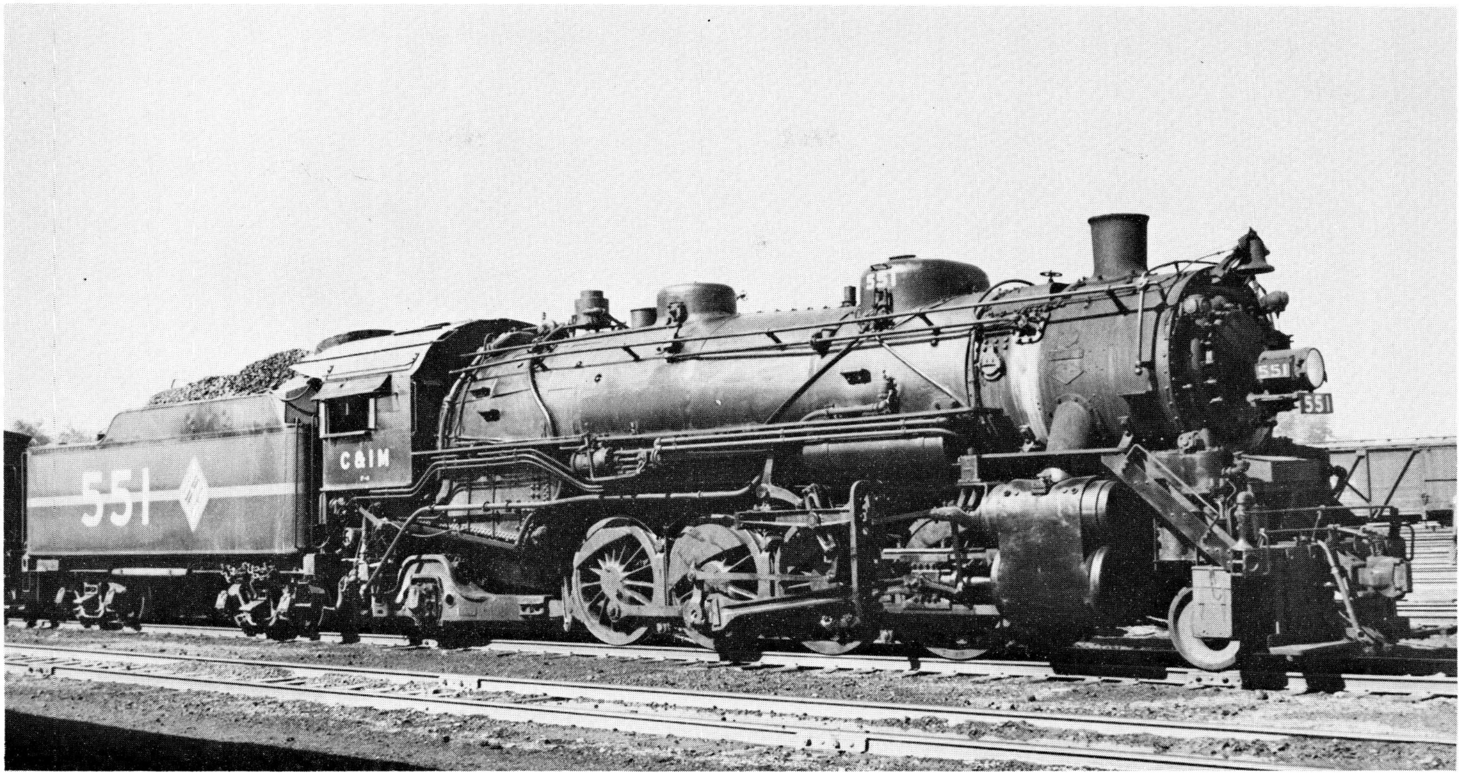
551
C&IM
551
551
551

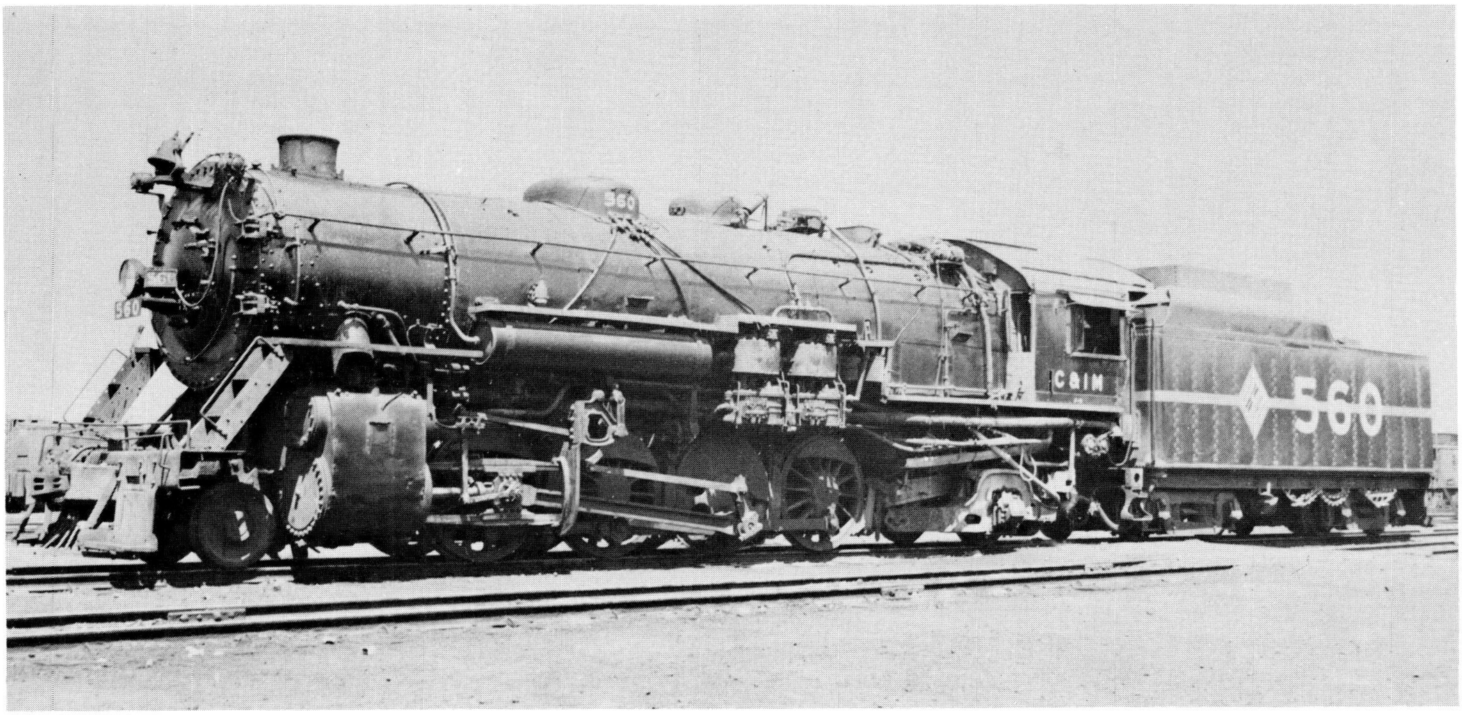
560
C&IM
560

In the final year of steam-powered passenger trains at Dearborn Station in Chicago — 1952 — Grand Trunk Western 4-8-4 No. 6405 was outstanding among the diesel-electric units of four other railroads. Built by Lima in 1938, they were almost identical with five others constructed by Montreal in 1936 for the Canadian National. [R. A. LeMassena]

Desperate for motive power to move the enormous tonnages of coal during World War II, the C&IM augmented its own fleet of eight 2-10-2's by purchasing 18 more from two other railroads. Numbers 600–603 came from Baldwin in 1927–1929. The 651–659 group was obtained from the Wabash. Lima produced the 700–703 group in 1931, and the Atlantic Coast Line sold the 751–759 series to the C&IM. [Four views: H. K. Vollrath Collection]

At least as far back as 1880, the Illinois Central operated a substantial commuter traffic to the south of Chicago. To haul these short trains, making frequent stops, the IC bought eight 2–4–4T's from Rogers during 1880–1883, Numbers 1401–1408, and then constructed Numbers 1409–1421 in its own shops during 1885–1891. A pair of 2–6–4T's, the 1422 and 1423, came from Rogers in 1892, as did the 1424–1433 — 2–4–6T's — during 1893–1895. From 1901–1904, the Illinois Central's shops rebuilt some 4–6–0's into 4–6–4T's, numbered 1434–1440. A final group of 2–6–4T's, numbered 1441–1456, were fabricated from old 2–6–0's in the 1912–1923 period. Most of these little locomotives were scrapped or sold in the late 1920's, when the IC electrified its suburban trackage and began operating multiple-unit electric cars. However, some of these engines were not retired until 1935. [C. W. Witbeck, I. W. Saunders, C. W. Witbeck, H. K. Vollrath Collection

1437
I.C.R.R.
SOUTH CHICAGO

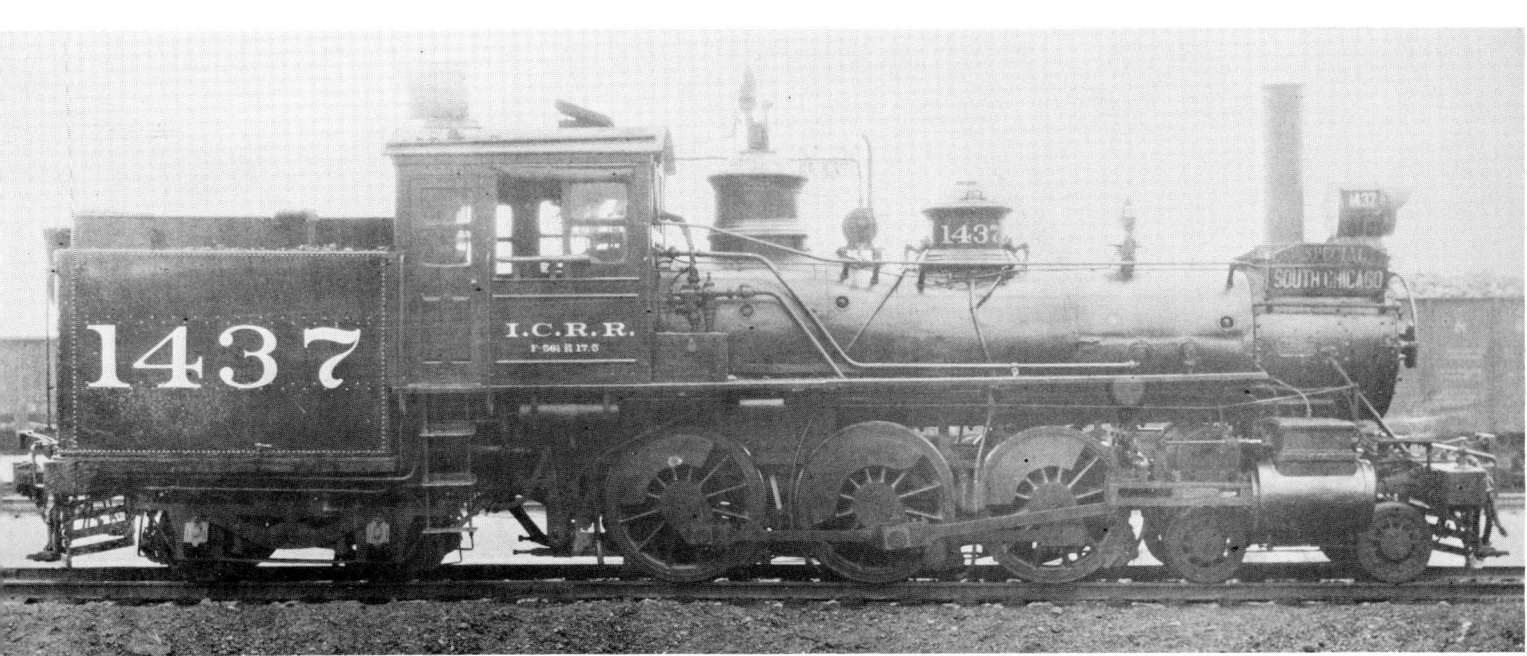

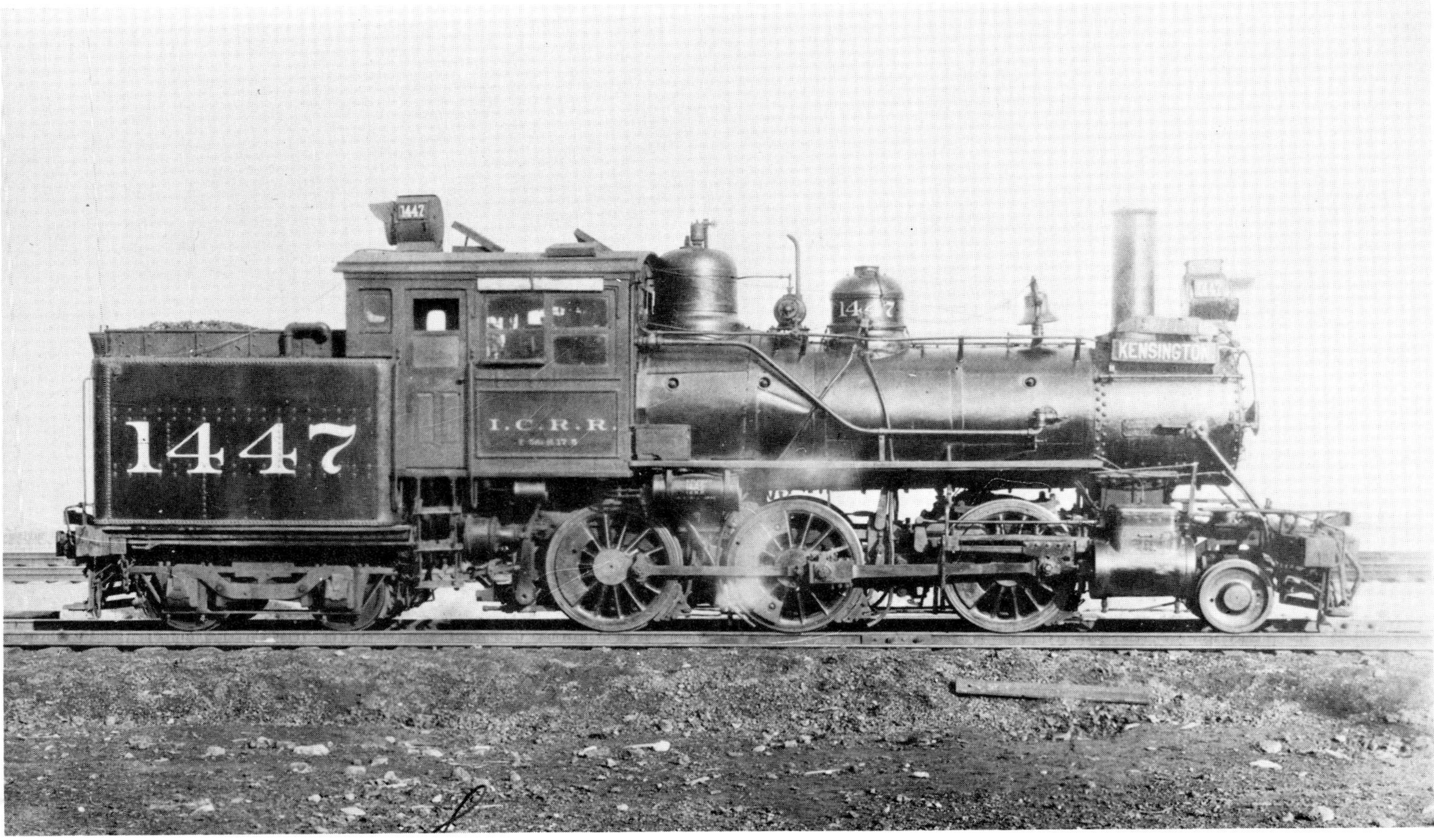
1447
I.C.R.R.
KENSINGTON

Because the Illinois Central's mainline was located parallel to the Mississippi River, its standard motive power for passenger service was the 4-6-2, nearly 200 of them delivered between 1905 and 1920. The 1145, delivered in 1916, was a typical example, which — like most of them — continued in service until the mid-1950's. [C. W. Burns]

Some 400 0–6–0's, constructed between 1889 and 1918, included several created in the Illinois Central's own shops by the removal of the pilot truck from old 2–6–0's. About half of them — those constructed after 1911 — were still operating in the early 1950's. [H. K. Vollrath Collection]

The IC's fleet of 0-8-0's consisted of 74 "normal" locomotives, numbered in the 3500 series, plus some interesting conversions. During World War II, the railroad's shops converted two groups of 2-8-0's into 0-8-0 switchers, numbered 3300–3330 and 3410–3424. (The 3401 had been the 3416.) No. 3499 possessed an odd appearance; it was the last of 50 old 2-8-2's, which became switchers by the amputation of both trucks [C. W. Burns Collection]

There were 517 new 2-8-2's at work on the Illinois Central, plus another 33, like the 3793, which had once been 2-8-0's. The conversions were performed in the IC's shops during the early 1920's. Another 26 came from two subsidiaries, which were absorbed in 1926. Finally, 41 more were fabricated from old 2-8-2 boilers mounted on modified 2-10-2 frames, between 1937 and 1942. Their rated tractive effort of 85,000 pounds (calculated) was not attained in actual service, due to the lack of weight on their drivers. [C. W. Burns, H. K. Vollrath Collection]

After the IC found that Lima's new 2-8-4 was superior to its 2-10-2's, it placed the biggest single order — 50 locomotives in 1926 — for that type. Between 1937 and 1940, these engines were rebuilt with smaller cylinders, greater steam pressure and Boxpok main drivers, but minus their Elesco feedwater heaters. Nearly all of them worked until 1955. [C. W. Burns Collection]

In 1937 the IC's shops took 2-8-4 No. 7038 and rebuilt it into a 4-6-4, and increased both steam pressure and driver diameter. Intended for fast-freight service, its performance was rather disappointing. Afterward, it was used in passenger service for about 10 years. [H. K. Vollrath Collection]

There were only seven 0-10-0 switchers in the Illinois Central's roster. The 3600 and 3601 had been acquired when the Alabama & Vicksburg was merged in 1926. They had been constructed by Baldwin in 1922 and 1924. The 3602–3606 had been A&V 2-10-2's, which were much smaller than the IC's 2-10-2's. [Both views: C. W. Burns Collection]

IC's fleet of 136 4-8-2's was the third largest, the first 60 having been delivered in 1923 and 1924. The railroad gave eight of them, Numbers 2300–2307, new boilers and cylinders with two valve chambers. Fifty-six more were constructed from older 2-10-2's during 1937–1942, Numbers 2500–2555. Another 20, numbered 2600–2619, were constructed in the railroad's shops during 1942–1943. Weighing 424,000 pounds, they were surpassed only by some rebuilt engines of the St. Louis-San Francisco Railroad. These locomotives were not retired until 1960. Two of the 2500's have been preserved. [Both views: C. W. Burns]

The Illinois Central created a new wheel arrangement by mounting boilers taken from old 2-8-2's on modified 2-10-2 chassis, the resulting combination being 2-10-0's, Numbers 3610–3624, which appeared between 1939 and 1941. [C. W. Burns]

The Illinois Central's first 2-10-2's, built by American in 1916 and 1918, were sold to the Central of Georgia in 1926; but at the end of 1923, the IC had received 125 bigger ones from Lima, numbered 2901–3025. Another five came from the Alabama & Vicksburg subsidiary in 1926. Then, commencing in 1939, 69 were rebuilt like the 2717, the last 20 having new boilers. [C. W. Burns Collection]

By 1926, the Central of Georgia — then an IC subsidiary — realized that it did not really need the 10 2-6+6-2's which it had purchased from American in 1919. So, it swapped them to the IC for seven 2-10-2's. The IC renumbered them 6000–6009, and put them to work in hump-yard service. [Unknown]

A fleet of 35 4-6-0's handled the New York, Chicago & St. Louis Railroad's passenger trains until the mid-1930's, when all but three had been retired, leaving only Numbers 156–158 to haul the Peoria, Illinois, branch runs. These had been delivered in 1913, and they continued in service until 1948. [R. A. LeMassena]

Heavier cars and longer trains were the reason behind the acquisition of 14 4-6-2's in 1923. The first four, Numbers 160–163, came from Lima; the others came from American. All of them worked until the early 1950's. [H. K. Vollrath Collection]

The NYC&StL's four 4-6-4's, Numbers 170–173, were delivered by American only one month after the first of that wheel arrangement had been erected for the New York Central in 1927. Lima built the next four in 1929, its first ones of that type. During World War II, they were operated with elongated tenders having a six-wheel front truck. Unstable at high speeds, these tenders were removed, replacing smaller ones on 2-8-2's. [R. A. LeMassena]

While the Nickel Plate's common switcher was the 0-6-0, the W&LE preferred the 0-8-0, the first five of which came from American in 1918. The W&LE copied the design, producing 20 more, numbered 5106–5125, in its own shops between 1928 and 1930. All of them were renumbered 271–295, but after only a couple of year's more service, about half were retired; yet, some of them — like the 292 — worked until 1956–1958. [C. W. Burns]

Freight was being hauled on the NYC&StL by a group of 106 2-8-2's constructed between 1917 and 1924. The 957 had been the 511, one of the earliest acquired. In striking contrast, the 668 displays the effect of continual modernization, which kept several of these locomotives useful until the late 1950's. Feedwater heaters, trailing-truck boosters, two airpumps and 12-wheel tenders made a remarkable transformation. [C. W. Burns, H. K. Vollrath Collection]

Like some other classes of Nickel Plate engines, the new NYC&StL 2-8-4's were produced by both American and Lima. Numbers 700–714 came from American's shops in 1934; Lima built the others, numbered 715–779, between 1942 and 1949, the 779 having been Lima's last steam locomotive. No. 702, eastbound through Frankfort, Indiana, in 1944, appears just as "new" as the 763, only a few months old when this photograph was taken at Conneaut, Ohio. [R. A. LeMassena, Ivan W. Saunders]

No. 846 possessed an unusual background. It was one of 10 4-8-2's constructed by the Norfolk & Western in 1926. All of them were sold during World War II to the Richmond, Fredericksburg & Potomac (6), and the Denver & Rio Grande Western (4), both of whom resold them to the Wheeling & Lake Erie. When the NYC&StL leased the W&LE in 1949, it inherited six of the big engines and renumbered them in the 840 series. The 840 was the last one remaining active — in 1953. [Unknown]

Hardly anyone knew that the NYC&StL operated four 2-6+6-2 Mallets, which had been numbered 8001–8003 and 8009 on the W&LE. Renumbered 940–943, they continued to haul coal in eastern Ohio until 1953, 37 years after their original delivery. [H. K. Vollrath Collection]

Owned by Republic Steel in Cleveland, Ohio, the River Terminal Railroad performed interchange and mill switching services. No. 47, bought from the St. Louis & O'Fallon — their No. 8 — as a 2-6-2, had been converted to an unusual 0-6-2. [I. W. Saunders]

Numbers 612–623 of the Wabash's fleet of 32 4–4–2's were given 84-inch drivers for high-speed passenger trains, but were replaced by 4–6–2's when their consists became too heavy. However, a few were retained for the *Detroit Arrow*, which ran between Chicago and Detroit, attaining speeds of 100 mph. enroute. [H. K. Vollrath Collection]

Only 16 of the 40 4-6-2's owned by the Wabash were new locomotives, Numbers 660–675. Those originals had been built by American and Baldwin in 1912, but had been modified by the addition of feedwater heaters and cast steel pilots. The 665 was approaching Chicago in 1947, when this portrait was made. [C. W. Burns]

Following the delivery of 4–8–4's in 1931, the Wabash never bought another new steam locomotive, but between 1943 and 1947, it took the boilers from 1923–1925-model 2–8–2's and mounted them on new 4–6–4 chassis. They replaced 4–6–2's in heavy passenger service on the mainlines. [C. W. Burns]

In 1925 the Wabash invested in a fleet of 50 2-8-2's, the last five of which had three cylinders, all of which were constructed by American. [H. K. Vollrath Collection]

The Wabash Railroad's newest-and-best motive power consisted of 25 very heavy 4-8-2's (406,000 pounds), built by Baldwin in 1930, and an equal number of 4-8-4's, also from Baldwin in 1930 and 1931, which were likewise quite heavy at that time (454,000 pounds). Their cylinders, driver diameters and tenders were identical, and their boilers differed only in steam pressure and grate area. Replacing 2-8-2's on mainline freight trains, they enabled the railroad to compete for fast-freight traffic. [H. K. Vollrath Collection, C. W. Jernstrom]

Lima's only contribution to Wabash motive power was a group of 0-8-0 switchers delivered in 1926, Numbers 1545–1569. American had built 20 similar ones in 1923. [H. K. Vollrath Collection]

Rather heavy for 2-10-2's when American erected them in 1917, the Wabash's 25 locomotives were intended for ordinary freight service. In one respect, they became an unique group; the railroad sold 23 of them to other railroads — two to the Chicago & Eastern Illinois, 10 to the Chicago & Illinois Midland, six to the Kansas City Southern, and five to the Missouri Pacific during World War II. [H. K. Vollrath Collection]

The Wheeling & Lake Erie's biggest passenger locomotive was the 4-4-2, six of which had been delivered by American — with 79-inch drivers — as Wabash Pittsburgh Terminal Numbers 2001–2006 in 1905. Almost immediately, they became W&LE Engines 2001–2006; then, they were renumbered as the 2301–2306 at the end of World War I. All six engines participated in the last passenger runs in 1938. On that occasion, No. 2301 was passing through Canton, Ohio. [C. W. Burns]

Between 1928 and 1940, the Wheeling & Lake Erie replaced its entire roster of switchers by building 30 0-6-0's, Numbers 3951–3980, and 20 0-8-0's, Numbers 5106–5125, all "improved" duplicates of the USRA standard designs. Six more 0-6-0's came from American in 1944. All of them went to the NYC&StL in 1949. [H. K. Vollrath Collection, C. W. Burns]

The road numbers given to W&LE engines indicated their tractive effort. The 4312, the last 2-8-0 acquired by the Wabash Pittsburgh Terminal — originally No. 2150, built by American in 1905 — was rated at 43,000 pounds. It was given its new number in 1918, and was rebuilt in 1928. The W&LE's last 2-8-0's were built by American in 1913 as Numbers 2401–2420, then, renumbered as 6051–6070 in 1918–1920. Weighing 275,000 pounds, the 6066 was among the heaviest of its type; it became Pittsburgh & West Virginia No. 951 in 1942. [Both views: C. W. Burns]

Numbers 6001–6020 were the W&LE's only 2-8-2's of USRA heavy design, constructed by American in 1918. After they went to the New York, Chicago & St. Louis Railroad in 1949, they were renumbered 671–690. [Both views: C. W. Burns]

Between 1937 and 1942, the W&LE acquired a fleet of 32 2-8-4's, all fabricated by American from plans for the Nickel Plate locomotives, but with some mechanical differences. They lacked the Worthington feedwater heaters; they had single-guide crossheads, Boxpok driver centers and footboard pilots. The 6404 was accelerating a coal train out of Harmon, junction of the W&LE's two mainlines. No. 6406 had just arrived — in 1937 — in Brewster, Ohio, and was being inspected by officials before its trial trip. The 6417 was headed northward through Canton, Ohio, with a trainload of coal. No. 6423 was hauling a merchandise train at Harmon in 1940. These engines were given Nickel Plate numbers 801–832 in 1952. [All four views: C. W. Burns]

In 1948 the W&LE brought together 10 ex-Norfolk & Western 4-8-2's, which had been sold to the Denver & Rio Grande Western (4) and the Richmond, Fredericksburg & Potomac (6) in 1945 and 1944. They became the 6801–6810; the 6804–6806, 6808 and the 6809 became NYC&StL Numbers 844–846, 848 and 849 in 1951, but they were all scrapped a couple of years later. [H. K. Vollrath Collection]

Like so many other coal-hauling railroads, the W&LE purchased Mallet-type locomotives to move the tonnages generated during World War I. Thus, in 1917, it received 20 2-6+6-2's from American, having quite unusual dimensions. Their cylinders, 25.5" and 39" x 32", were the same as those of 2-8+8-2's, and their 63-inch drivers were exceeded only by a pair of Baltimore & Ohio engines built in 1930. At 200 psi. boiler pressure, their tractive effort was 81,000 pounds; and during the mid-1920's it became 88,000 pounds when the pressure was raised to 220 psi. Originally, the 8401–8420 had two airpumps on the left side; they were subsequently moved to the smokebox front, as illustrated by the 8401, and as the 8412 shows, they were replaced by compound compressors. Because their 99 square feet grate area was so large, outside ashpans were installed. The 8413 was dragging a coal train into Brewster, Ohio, in 1938. Ten more USRA standard Mallets came from Baldwin in 1919, but they were smaller in every aspect. All of the 8400's were dismantled in 1939, but four of the 8001–8010 group were still running when the NYC&StL took over the W&LE in 1949. [All four views: C. W. Burns]

No. 1214 was one of the Norfolk & Western's improved 2-6+6-4's, having a tractive effort of 134,000 pounds and 6,700 DBHP at 35 mph. In this portrait the engine was hauling a long train of empty coal cars westbound, approaching the summit of the steep grade up to Blue Ridge, Virginia. [E. P. Street, Jr.]

# Chapter V

## NORTHERN SOUTHLAND

Chesapeake & Ohio
Clinchfield
East Tennessee & Western North Carolina
Interstate
Norfolk Southern
Norfolk & Western
Tennessee & North Carolina
Virginian
Winston-Salem Southbound

The territorial band embracing the northernmost states of the "South" spanned the widest part of the Appalachian Mountains, where there were enormous deposits of soft coal. Three railroads, Chesapeake & Ohio; Norfolk & Western; Virginian, brought the coal from the mines to concentration yards where solid trainloads were dispatched to destinations along the Atlantic Coast, or westward into the vast industrial region north of the Ohio River. Train tonnages were incredibly large: 10,000–15,000 tons being normal. The gradients between originating yards and terminals were so severe that the most powerful locomotives were constructed to haul the trains. Double-heading, with a rear-end helper, became standard practice, and both the Virginian and Norfolk & Western electrified their most difficult mainline segments. The Clinchfield (owned by the Louisville & Nashville and Atlantic Coast Line railroads), Interstate (owned by the Virginia Coal & Iron Company), and Winston-Salem Southbound (owned by the Norfolk & Western and Atlantic Coast Line railroads) provided secondary routes for the movement of coal.

The four railroads which offered passenger service, Clinchfield, Virginian, Chesapeake & Ohio, and Norfolk & Western, utilized 4-6-2's on their passenger trains, though the C&O and N&W also had 4-8-2's for their mountain trackage. After 1935, the C&O began to use 4-8-4's, then 4-6-4's and 2-8-4's in the late 1940's. The N&W designed and built an extremely powerful 4-8-4, and commenced operations with them in 1941. For freight haulage, the motive-power philosophies of the C&O, N&W and VGN differed greatly. The VGN first acquired 2-6+6-0's, then went to 2-8+8-2's and some 2-10+10-2's. After a gap of 22 years, it purchased a few 2-6+6-6's like those of the C&O. The N&W acquired the largest group of 4-8-0's, added a fleet of 2-6+6-2's, and constructed the most efficient and powerful compound-expansion 2-8+8-2's. Its single-expansion 2-6+6-4's were surpassed only by the C&O's mammoth 2-6+6-6's, that railroad's ultimate locomotive. The C&O's roster included the largest group of 2-6+6-2's, a great many huge 2-8-2's, 2-8-4's and 2-10-4's, and the first fleet of single-expansion 2-8+8-2's. Precipitously, and almost simultaneously, the steam era ended during 1958.

For its two end-to-end daily passenger trains, the Clinchfield used 4-6-2's so old that their Walschaerts valve gear required a special mechanism to move the valves, which were located inside the frames. Note the unusual headlight position. [C. W. Burns Collection]

Some of the Clinchfield Railroad's 2-8-2's — like No. 499 — were veritable rolling antiques with slide-valve cylinders and archbar trucks beneath their tenders. Management must have felt that these engines would last forever. [C. W. Burns Collection]

By Clinchfield's criteria, the 411 was a rather modern 2-8-2, used for local freight service. Yes, it does have a headlight. [C. W. Burns Collection]

Until the arrival of these 4-6+6-4's in 1942, the Clinchfield had not acquired a new engine in 18 years. Designed more for fast-freight service than coal drags, these engines would have been more suitable for the Clinchfield's steep grades had they been 2-8+8-2's. Incidentally, they were the only such locomotives with Baker valve gear. [C. W. Burns Collection]

In 1947 the Clinchfield got a bargain by purchasing the six Union Pacific-design 4-6+6-4's, which had been leased by the Federal government to the Denver & Rio Grande Western during World War II. They received Numbers 670–675 and worked until the end of steam in 1955. [C. W. Burns Collection]

When a Chesapeake & Ohio 2-8-4 brought a train into Elkhorn City, Kentucky, it was unable to pull the consist up the steep grade into the yard. Consequently, the Clinchfield engine assisted it for the last mile. The locomotives are C&O No. 2775 and Clinchfield No. 663, American Locomotive Company's last articulated. [B. F. Cutler]

After acquiring 21 2–6+6–2's between 1909 and 1916, the Clinchfield Railroad had Baldwin construct seven 2–8+8–2's with unusually large cylinders. Also, the application of Baker valve gear was not common at that time, except for the USRA standard locomotives. [C. W. Burns Collection]

The coal-traffic boom following World War I caused the CC&O to purchase 10 USRA-design 2-8+8-2's from Baldwin in 1919, then another 10 near-duplicates from American in 1923. Another 18 years would elapse before the railroad bought any new locomotives. [C. W. Burns Collection]

The Chesapeake & Ohio operated only 20 4-4-2's, all constructed by American between 1902 and 1907. They were rebuilt in the early 1920's with new frames, cylinders and valve gear. As they became less useful on local runs, they were concentrated on the Chicago Branch, where they ended their service in 1949. [B. F. Cutler]

The acquisition of the Hocking Valley in 1930 brought a small group of 4-6-0's — numbered 86–92 — into the C&O's roster of motive power. They were not needed elsewhere on the system; so, they remained in their original assignments — passenger runs between Athens and Toledo, Ohio. [B. F. Cutler]

The Chesapeake & Ohio's last 10 0-6-0's, whose final numbers were 25–34, were bought from American in 1905 specifically for transfer runs between Cincinnati, Ohio, and Covington, Kentucky. By 1952, diesel-electric units had replaced all of the smaller switchers, and these were the last to go. [C. W. Burns Collection]

After the C&O had acquired its "last" steam locomotives in 1948, it purchased three "fireless" (steam-storage) locomotives from Porter in 1949 for hazardous industrial switching in South Charleston, West Virginia. Ironically, these engines kept the C&O from being 100-percent diesel for many years — until the late 1960's. [H. K. Vollrath Collection]

In 1948, the Chesapeake & Ohio received a massive influx of new locomotives, including 4–6–4's, 2–8–4's, 4–8–4's, 2–6+6–6's and 30 0–8–0's, bringing the total of that type to 210 engines. Yet, two years later, in its rush to convert to internal-combustion motive power, the railroad sold all 30 of the 0–8–0's to the Norfolk & Western, and 15 Lima-built (1942) engines to the Virginian. [H. K. Vollrath Collection]

The C&O was one of the few railroads to use the 0–10–0 switcher. It bought 15 of them during 1919–1921 and used them in coal-train marshalling yards. Eventually, they congregated in Peach Creek Yard, where some were still working in 1956. [H. K. Vollrath Collection]

Seventeen 4-6-2's joined C&O ranks when the Pere Marquette Railroad was merged into the system in 1947, but only a few were actually renumbered for continued service on C&O trackage. [H. K. Vollrath Collection]

One of the earliest purchasers of the 4-6-2 wheel arrangement, the C&O added to its fleet until 1926, and then modified the older ones and rebuilt the newer engines, like the 473. With its enormous tender, early-pattern Boxpok driving wheels and Worthington feedwater heater, the engine's age is betrayed only by its original valve-gear frame. [I. W. Saunders]

Following World War II, the C&O needed more secondary-line passenger power; so, it bought four of the Richmond, Fredericksburg & Potomac's 1927-model 4–6–2's, which were among the heaviest of that type. They were assigned to the Louisville, Kentucky, branch, where gradients were 2.7 percent. [H. K. Vollrath Collection]

To relieve its 4-6-2's of rapidly increasing traffic prior to World War II, the Chesapeake & Ohio ordered eight of the largest 4-6-4's ever built. One could say that the 2-8-4's boiler and firebox was mounted on a 4-6-4 chassis. Baldwin delivered the 300–307 in early 1942, and they were immediately put to work on the more level trackage at the extremities of the system. Five more, numbered 310–314 and equipped with poppet valves, were delivered in 1948. [C. W. Burns Collection]

Beneath the grimy exterior of the 542, at Chicago in 1947, was one of the first three 4-8-2's, erected by American in 1911 and 1912. Its by-pass valves, indirect valve gear, inside-bearing trailing truck and outside ashpans attest to its age, despite the large cylindrical tender, two compound airpumps and new cab. [C. W. Burns]

The seven USRA heavy 4-8-2's, acquired by the C&O in 1918–1923, were vastly different — and superior — from those delivered previously. In every aspect, they were bigger. After a late-1930's rebuilding, they were so visibly different that only the Cole trailing truck and the old-model valve-gear frame were recognizable. Displaced by 4-8-4's from the more difficult assignments, they handled heavy passenger trains on the Washington, D.C., line until 1952. [C. W. Burns Collection]

It was common practice for the C&O to assign 2-8-4's to passenger trains on its divisions with steep grades. In this scene at Clifton Forge, Virginia, 4-8-4 No. 600 and 2-8-4 No. 2740 were accelerating the Sportsman eastbound toward Charlottesville. [R. A. LeMassena]

The 971 was the typical freight engine before the bigger engines began to arrive. Constructed between 1903 and 1907, many of them worked on branchlines until the mid-1950's. Meanwhile, most of them had been rebuilt at least once. This example was still at work in Chicago in 1948. [C. W. Burns]

No. 1106, delivered by American in 1911, was among the oldest of the C&O's 2-8-2's, as might be inferred from its inside-bearing trailing truck. Despite its age, this locomotive was still able to haul a train of 150 coal-laden hoppers at Toledo, Ohio. [W. R. Osborne]

Over a two-year period, 1924–1926, the Chesapeake & Ohio acquired 150 heavy 2-8-2's to haul coal after it had been brought out of the mountainous mining areas. No. 1199 had been given a much larger tender, but it has lost its feedwater heater and trailing-truck booster. [C. W. Burns]

Because its 2-8-2's were so successful, the C&O did not acquire the 2-8-4 type until 1943, 18 years after its introduction, and then it purchased 90 of them between 1943 and 1948, adding another 40 when the Pere Marquette was absorbed. Though they displaced the 2-8-2's everywhere, and were regularly assigned to passenger service, they were doomed to premature retirement by the arrival of diesel-electric units, and all of them had been idled by 1957. [H. K. Vollrath Collection]

Almost a decade elapsed after the delivery of the first 4-8-4, before the Chesapeake & Ohio purchased its first ones, from Lima in 1935. However, they were enormous locomotives, having 100-inch diameter boilers, 100 square feet of grate area and a weight barely exceeded by only two others in the East. The 610–614 group were Lima's last, delivered in 1948. No. 614 has been preserved and is operational. [C. W. Burns Collection]

The C&O's 15 0-10-0's were utilized to make up long loaded coal trains in relatively level concentration yards. Their final days found them at Peach Creek, West Virginia, where they worked until their replacement by diesel-electric units in 1956. [R. R. Malinoski]

On the following two pages: Every one of the C&O's 2-10-2's was second-hand, the consequence of two mergers and the desperate need for wartime locomotives. After various mechanical modifications, they were given larger tenders and were assigned to heavy transfer work in yards at Washington, D.C., Russell, Kentucky, and Toledo, Ohio. No. 2003 was purchased from the Chicago & Eastern Illinois in 1945. [W. C. Witbeck] Numbers 2952 and 2953 had been built for the Lehigh Valley, which sold them to the Hocking Valley, absorbed by the C&O in 1930. [W. C. Witbeck] The 2987 had been built for the Pere Marquette, which was merged into the C&O in 1947. [H. K. Vollrath Collection] No. 4001 had been sold by the Wabash to the C&EI, which resold it to the C&O in 1945. [C. W. Burns Collection]

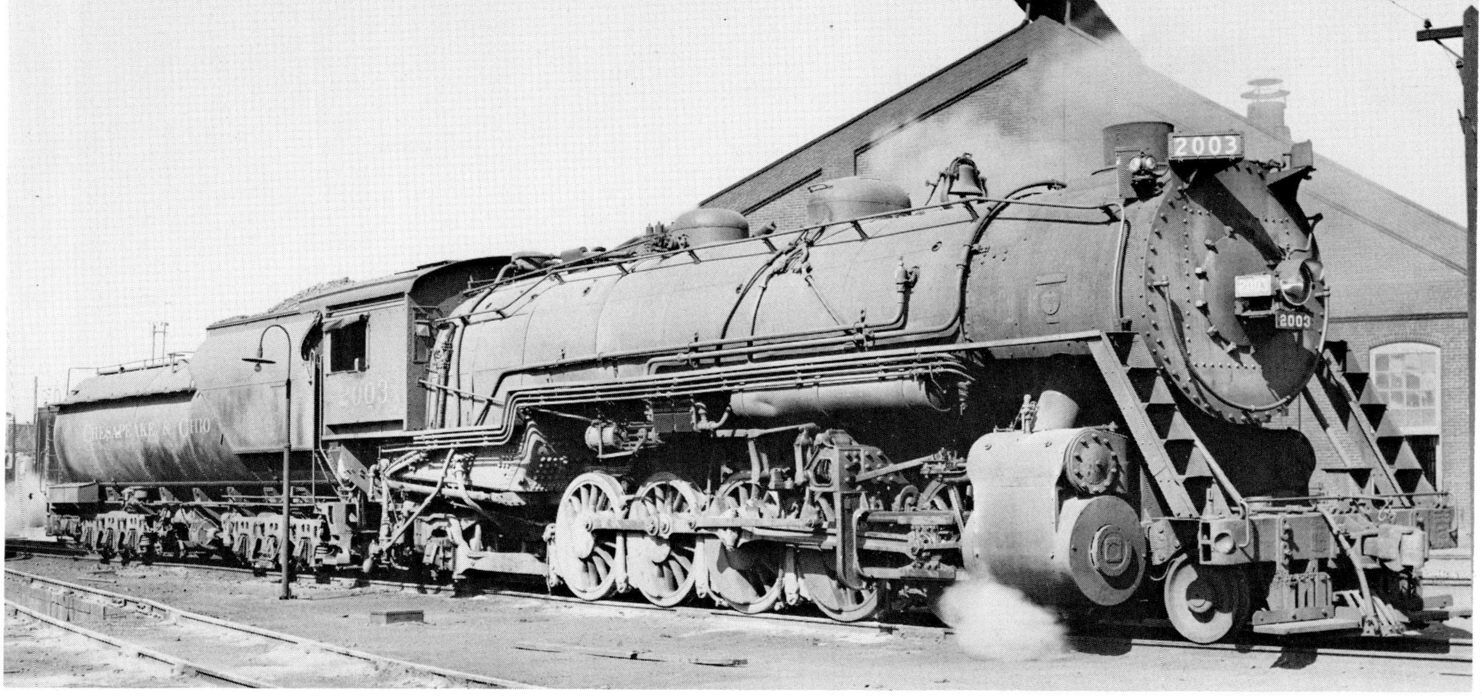
2003
CHESAPEAKE & OHIO
2003

2952
2952

2953
CHESAPEAKE & OHIO
2953

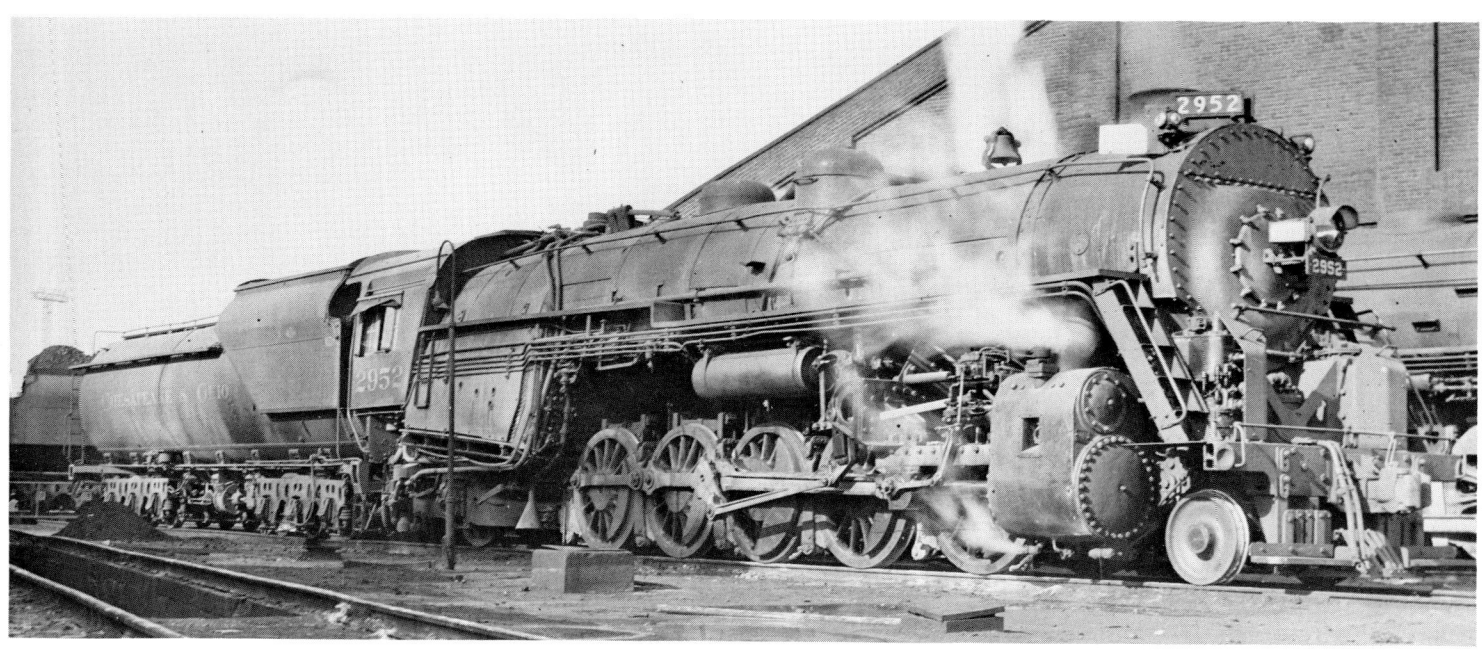

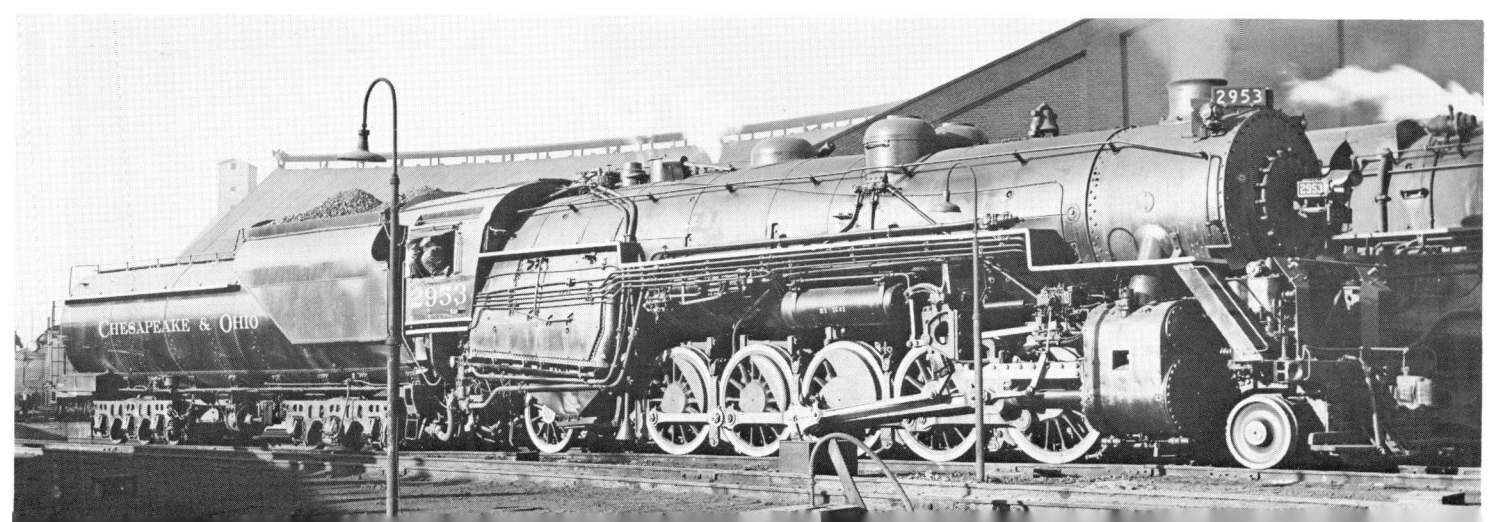

The 2-10-4's, delivered by Lima in 1930, were most remarkable locomotives. Designed with large boilers, large fireboxes and cylinders, and equipped with a trailing-truck booster, they could start the same train as the single-expansion 2-8+8-2's acquired only fours years earlier, and their larger drivers enabled them to run much faster. Their engine-and-tender weight was an incredible 981,000 pounds. [C. T. Foster]

Several of the C&O's fleet of 2-6+6-2's, No. 1275–1299, had come from the Hocking Valley in 1930, and they were essentially identical with contemporary C&O Mallets. After the merger they remained on HV trackage, running from coal mines in southeastern Ohio to Toledo. [C. W. Burns]

The 10 2-6+6-2 Mallets, which were delivered in 1949, were not only the C&O's last steam locomotives, but also were Baldwin's last articulateds and the last conventional steam locomotive erected by a commercial builder for a U.S. railroad. The 1309 was the final one, photographed after having been exhibited at the Chicago Railroad Fair in 1949. [M. D. McCarter]

During 1927, No. 1470, a standard compound-expansion 2-6+6-2, was rebuilt in the C&O's shops to single-expansion and equipped with a front-end throttle. Evidently, the improvement in performance was not worth the extra expense because it was never duplicated. [H. K. Vollrath Collection]

Even though the 2-10-4's were excellent locomotives, the C&O wanted something with greater tractive effort, horsepower and flexibility for hauling freight trains across the mountains between Hinton, West Virginia, and Clifton Forge, Virginia. Lima built 60 gigantic 2-6+6-6's between 1941 and 1948, each weighing 1,200,000 pounds and capable of delivering 8,000 drawbar-horsepower. They were Lima's last articulateds, of which this one — the 1601 — has been preserved. [R. A. LeMassena]

When they were delivered in 1924 and 1926, the 45 single-expansion 2-8+8-2 Mallets were revolutionary locomotives. They displaced 2-6+6-2's on the mainline over the mountains, handling longer trains in less time. Eventually, their 57-inch drivers became a handicap, and when the 2-6+6-6's began to arrive, they were re-assigned or sold to other railroads. The first 25 locomotives, built by American, had an unusual valve-gear arrangement, direct Walschaerts on the front engine, indirect on the rear. [Unknown]

During World War II the C&O sold 30 2-8+8-2's to the Union Pacific, which modified 11 of them per the accompanying photograph. Three others were sold to the Richmond, Fredericksburg & Potomac for hump-yard work at Alexandria, Virginia. No. 3 shows only minor modifications. [C. W. Burns, H. K. Vollrath Collection]

Other major railroads purchased Shay-type locomotives for special purposes, but the C&O possessed the largest group, a total of 17, including 15 of the four-truck model, like No. 12. They were used on the steep-and-winding coal branches southeast of Charleston, West Virginia, until 1913. [H. K. Vollrath Collection]

In the far western toe of Virginia was a virtually unknown railroad whose motive power was derived from its owners. Its four big 2-8-0's had come from the Southern Railway. These were the Southern's biggest, weighing 246,000 pounds, purchased by the Interstate Railroad in 1952, after 26 years of service on the Southern. [H. K. Vollrath Collection]

Who would expect to find a pair of ex-Pennsylvania 2-8-2's working in the mountains of western Virginia? Interstate Numbers 14 and 15 were purchased from the PRR in 1948. [H. K. Vollrath Collection]

During World War II, the Interstate obtained three 2-6+6-2 Mallets, numbered 22–24, from the Norfolk & Western. However, they were not used very long, and all were gone by 1950. [R. E. Prince]

After World War I, the demand for coal caused the Interstate to buy a pair of USRA standard 2-8+8-2's to move its trains over 2.5-percent grades and 18-degree curves. These big Mallets worked for almost 35 years before being replaced by diesel-electric locomotives. [R. E. Prince]

Just as its name stated, the East Tennessee & Western North Carolina's narrow-gauge track extended from Elizabethton to ancient iron mines at Cranberry. Although its passenger-service days had ended long ago, 4-6-0 No. 12 was handling switching chores at Elizabethton in 1947. Note the interesting coupler, capable of joining with cars of both gauges. [R. A. LeMassena]

During 1940, the Norfolk Southern purchased five tiny 2-8-4's from Baldwin, the smallest of that type. With loaded tender, these locomotives weighed less than 600,000 pounds. After working for only a decade on the NS, they were sold to the American Smelting & Refining Company (ASARCO), which operated serveral mines in Mexico, but they bore National Railways of Mexico (NdeM) numbers 3350–3354. Then, as ASARCO accumulated bills for freight charges, it applied them against the cost of the engines. [Unknown]

By 1916, the Norfolk & Western Railway had retired all of its antiquated 0-6-0's and 0-8-0's (made from old 2-8-0's), except for a few 0-8-0 tank engines used for moving dead locomotives at major terminals. The 902 was a typical example. [H. K. Vollrath Collection]

Finally, in 1950, two years after the last 0-8-0's had been built (for the Chesapeake & Ohio), the N&W purchased all 30 of those switchers, and then they began to construct 45 more in their own shops. The last one, No. 244, erected in 1953, was the last reciprocating steam locomotive built for a U.S. common-carrier railroad. [H. K. Vollrath Collection]

Passenger trains on the N&W were hauled by 57 rather old 4-6-2's, which were acquired between 1905 and 1914, and even the arrival of 4-8-2's did not cause their demise. Five more, of 1913 vintage, were obtained from the Pennsylvania Railroad in 1930 to haul fast passenger trains out of Norfolk, Virginia. Having 80-inch drivers, they were superior to the N&W engines with 70-inch wheels. The N&W modified them, gave them large 12-wheel tenders, and numbered them 500–504. [Both photos: H. K. Vollrath Collection]

Awaiting the conductor's signal to commence its 90 mph. run with the *Powhatan Arrow* westbound from Norfork, Virginia, streamlined 4-8-4 No. 603 shows little evidence of its ability to produce 5,300 DBHP at high speeds with heavy trains. [R. A. LeMassena]

Like so many other coal-hauling railroads, the Norfolk & Western amassed a substantial collection of 2–8–0's, the newest of which was delivered in 1905. Thus, it is remarkable that some of these ancient locomotives were still being operated after 1950. [H. K. Vollrath Collection]

The 2-8-0 was quickly found to be inadequate for moving the increasingly heavy coal trains; consequently, the N&W began to buy 4-8-0's from American and Baldwin in 1906, and completed their unequalled fleet of that type by building 11, like No. 1153, in their own shops during 1911 and 1912. Several of these engines were used on branch lines, and they were not retired until the late 1950's. [H. K. Vollrath Collection]

Having disposed of its old 0-6-0 and 0-8-0 switchers, the N&W began to use 4-8-0's and 2-6+6-2 Mallets for yard work. In 1947, two 4-8-0's were modified for one-man operation, an experiment which was abandoned after a couple of years of operational testing. [H. K. Vollrath Collection]

Despite the adverse grades and severe curvature on its mainlines, the N&W did not immediately embrace the 4–8–2 wheel arrangement which had been introduced in 1911 on the Chesapeake & Ohio. However, the N&W undertook the erection of 16 locomotives in its shops, Numbers 100–115, during 1916 and 1917. And to handle World War I traffic, it obtained 10 more of USRA-standard heavy design from American in 1919. Four years later, it bought 10 duplicates from Baldwin. After World War II, the railroad completely rebuilt the first group, giving them integral cast-steel beds and cylinders, Worthington feedwater heaters and bigger 12-wheel tenders obtained from the C&O. The 116–137 group were similarly rebuilt, then given streamlined shrouding and 30-ton, 22,000-gallon tenders. Most of the 4–8–2's were still running in 1958, and some were not retired until 1959, at the end of the steam era on the N&W. [Both views: H. K. Vollrath Collection]

In 1926, the weights of 4-8-2's exceeded 400,000 pounds for the first time on the Baltimore & Ohio, and the Denver & Rio Grande Western, as well as on the Norfolk & Western, when the railroad erected Numbers 200–209 in their own shops. These engines were notable for their enormous boilers and fireboxes, and the N&W engines had small drivers, 63 inches in diameter. They handled freight trains between Roanoke and Norfolk, Virginia; however, because they did not run well above 35 miles per hour, they were sold to the Richmond, Fredricksburg & Potomac (Numbers 200–205) in 1944, and to the D&RGW (Numbers 206–209) in 1945. [Two upper views: H. K. Vollrath Collection, lower view: J. Schick]

Instead of adding more of the big Mallets, the N&W began to acquire a fleet of compound-expansion 2-6+6-2's in 1912, and by 1918, the railroad owned 190 such engines, built by American and Baldwin, Numbers 1300–1489. Commencing in 1926, the N&W's shops rebuilt 74 of these locomotives, giving them piston-valve low-pressure cylinders, Worthington feedwater heaters and tenders of much greater capacity. Although these smaller Mallets were no longer suitable for mainline traffic, they were useful for local freight, branchline and yard-switching work, and some of them were still active in 1957. No. 1399 was rebuilt to single expansion, but there was no significant improvement in performance to justify the cost. [Baldwin Locomotive Works, W. E. Warden, Norfolk & Western Railway]

During World War II, the N&W sold 10 of its 2-6+6-2's to other railroads — one to the Winston-Salem Southbound; two to the Denver & Rio Grande Western; three to the Interstate; and four to the Tennessee Central. This photograph shows Denver & Rio Grande Western No. 3351. [R. H. Kindig, R. J. Foster]

Because of its mountainous profile and unhurried passenger schedules, the N&W was — surprisingly — among the last railroads to utilize the 4-8-4 type, which had been so successful elsewhere since its introduction in 1926. World War II was the catalyst which caused the railroad to build five of them in 1941, and they were exceptional locomotives. They had a grate area of 108 square feet, a boiler diameter of 102 inches, and the longest combustion chamber applied to a 4-8-4, 102 inches. With 300 psi. steam pressure, they developed 5,300 drawbar-horsepower, and although their drivers were quite small — 70 inches in diameter — they experienced no difficulties in running well over 100 miles per hour. The final one, No. 613, was the last 4-8-4 built in the U.S.A.; and No. 611, which has been preserved, pulled the N&W's last steam-powered passenger train in 1958. [H. K. Vollrath Collection]

More than once, because of a mainline wreck, the N&W rerouted passenger trains over the electrified line of the Virginian Railway west of Roanoke, Virginia. This train was the eastbound Pocahontas, pulled by 4-8-4 No. 601. [H. W. Pontin]

As the nation began to emerge from the severe economic depression of the 1930's, the N&W realized it did not possess adequate motive power to handle fast-freight trains. In addition to that, the railroad's huge 2-8+8-2's were not suitable for higher speeds on nearly level track. Once again, the railroad's designers produced an incredible locomotive — one having 300 psi. of steam pressure, 121 square feet of grate area, a 106-inch boiler diameter and 70-inch drivers. This monster locomotive was capable of developing 6,300 drawbar-horsepower in the 30–40 miles-per-hour range, and it could be operated at passenger-train speeds. The first two of these 2-6+6-4's, numbered 1200 and 1201, were completed in 1936. No. 1206 was exhibited at the 1939 Worlds Fair in New York City; No. 1223, ready to depart Crewe, Virginia, was a later version of the 2-6+6-4, as indicated by the pilot, crossheads and tender. [R. A. LeMassena, C. W. Jernstrom]

The final five locomotives, Nos. 1238–1942, embodied even more improvements to increase drawbar horsepower (6,700 h.p.) and tractive effort (134,000 pounds). All axles and driving rods were equipped with roller bearings, and needle bearings were installed in the valve gear. No. 1238 was photographed when it was erected in 1949; the 1240 was making a final trip with an excursion in July of 1959; and only a month later, all six locomotives still operating were retired. No. 1218 was preserved, and is now hauling special excursions. [Norfolk & Western Railway, C. W. Jernstrom]

Realizing that 4–8–0's were not a satisfactory solution to its problem of moving ever-greater tonnages of coal, the N&W bought five 0–8+8–0 Mallets in 1910, Numbers 990–994, from American, and five 2–8+8–2's from Baldwin, Numbers 995–999. In their basic dimensions, these locomotives were alike; steam pressure, grate area, cylinder size, driver diameter, weight on drivers and tractive effort. Neither proved to be completely satisfactory, however. The Baldwins were retired in 1924; the 0–8+8–0's worked as yard switchers until 1934. [American Locomotive Company, Baldwin Locomotive Works]

By the time the last 2-6+6-2 Mallets had arrived, N&W's shops had begun to erect a much larger 2-8+8-2, whose design utilized the chassis of the Baldwin Mallet, supporting a much larger boiler and firebox. By 1924, 11 had been completed, Numbers 1700–1710; however, during 1919, Baldwin delivered 20 duplicates. Fifteen of these engines were sold to the D&RGW during World War II, and two more went to the Utah Copper Company, which modified them in almost unrecognizable fashion. [H. K. Vollrath Collection, G. V. Smith]

Excepting only a steam-turbine electric locomotive, the 2050–2089 series of USRA-duplicate 2-8+8-2's were the last new engines purchased by the Norfolk & Western. American delivered them to the railroad in 1927. The N&W installed Worthington feedwater heaters and relocated the airpumps soon after the 2050–2079 group to conform to the last 10 of the series. Five of them were given 8-8 tenders, obtained from the Atlantic Coast Line, like the one attached to No. 2083. No. 2050 has been preserved. [C. W. Jernstrom]

During 1919, the N&W received 50 USRA-design 2-8+8-2's, 45 from American and 5 from Baldwin, Numbers 2000–2049. Their chassis was almost identical with that of the 1700's, but the boiler was redesigned for improved combustion and steam production. As the photographs of No. 2009 indicate, these engines were modified extensively by the N&W. During World War II, 19 of them were sold to the Atchison, Topeka & Sante Fe (8); Pennsylvania (6); and Union Pacific (5); however, most of those remaining were still working in 1958. [Norfolk & Western Railway, [Two views: H. K. Vollrath Collection, C. W. Burns]

N&W 2-8+8-2 No. 2196 represented the ultimate achievement in steam locomotive design. All engine and tender axles were equipped with roller bearings; the smokebox was insulated. The booster valve had been installed (above the rear cylin-

der), and the low-pressure cylinders had been modified. An old tender had been added to eliminate stopping for water enroute. [Norfolk & Western Railway]

In 1931, the Norfolk & Western began the fabrication of 2-8+8-2's embodying improvements in every aspect of design and construction, beginning with No. 2101 and ending with No. 2200 in 1952, three years after the commercial builders had delivered their final steam locomotives to common-carrier railroads in North America. They established new records for efficiency, speed, drawbar-pull, reliability and operating costs. Their steam pressure was 300 psi.; their driver diameter was 58 inches; but their grate area of 106 square feet and cylinder dimensions of 25" and 39" x 32" remained the same, though their valve diameters were enlarged. Their tenders, loaded with 30 tons of coal and 22,000 gallons of water, weighed 378,000 pounds — the engine alone having weighed 612,000 pounds. These locomotives were operated until the final days of steam on the N&W; the last one, No. 2191, ran until May of 1960. No. 2156 has been preserved. [Three views: C. W. Jernstrom;

In 1907, three years before the N&W acquired its first Mallet, the railroad purchased a gigantic four-truck Shay geared locomotive weighing 336,000 pounds. This engine worked out of Bluefield, West Virginia, on the steep, curving branches to coal mines and lumber mills in the mountainous country, a task it performed well until it was sold in 1916. [Norfolk & Western Railway]

Until 1950, when the Virginian bought 15 1942-1943-model switchers from the Chesapeake & Ohio, numbered 240–254 on both railroads, it possessed only five such engines, all built in 1909 and 1910. No. 2 ran until 1955, and No. 4 was set aside for preservation in 1957. [S. P. Davidson, H. K. Vollrath Collection]

The Virginian's Charleston (West Virginia)-Roanoke-Norfolk (Virginia) daily passenger train required six 4-6-2's, numbered 210–215, and built in 1920 by American. This was the eastbound train, ready to depart Charleston in the morning. [R. A. LeMassena]

Over a period of 34 years, the VGN did not purchase any motive power except articulateds and electric locomotives. Then, in 1946, it acquired five Lima 2-8-4's, numbered 505–509, to replace the not-fast-enough rebuilt 2-8-2's between Norfolk and Roanoke, Virginia. They were duplicates of contemporary Chesapeake & Ohio locomotives. [H. K. Vollrath Collection]

Having little use for 2–8–0's, the Virginian invested in a substantial fleet of 2–8–2's, the newest of which were built by Baldwin in 1909–1912, Numbers 420–479. Five of them were rebuilt by the railroad, and then renumbered 480–484. The 468 was assisting a detoured N&W passenger train up the 2.1-percent grade east of Elmore, West Virginia. [H. W. Pontin, H. K. Vollrath Collection]

In common with other lumbering railroads, the Tennessee & North Carolina operated with a minimum of customary facilities. In this scene, its three-truck Shay locomotive, No. 80, was replenishing its water supply from a line-side creek. [R. A. LeMassena]

After buying the first 12 2-6+6-0's in 1909–1910, the Virginian acquired six monstrous 2-8+8-2's having low-pressure cylinders 44 inches in diameter, boilers 112 inches in diameter and 99 square feet of grate area. They worked on the two-percent grade from Elmore to Clarks Gap, West Virginia, hauling solid trains of coal, until their retirement in the early 1930's. [Cecil Cook Collection]

After testing an unsuccessful triplex steam locomotive, the Virginian ordered the only new 2-10+10-2's from American in 1918. They had the largest cylinders ever given to any locomotive — 48 inches in diameter — and a 119-inch-diameter boiler, with a grate area of 109 square feet. When starting, with high-pressure steam being admitted to all four cylinders, the tractive effort was 177,000 pounds, and it was 147,000 pounds after changing over to compound operation. No. 800, which bore American's Construction No. 60,000, was the last one to be retired — in 1952. [S. P. Davidson]

The six 2-8+8-2's and 10 2-10+10-2's were so occupied on the two-percent hill eastward from Elmore that the railroad obtained 20 more 2-8+8-2's to cope with increased coal traffic elsewhere. American constructed them to USRA standard design in 1919, giving them numbers 701–720. They weighed the same as the previous Mallets, but they had higher steam pressure and smaller cylinders. This one was the 704, drifting down the two-percent grade near Page, West Virginia. [S. P. Davidson]

Another 15 USRA 2-8+8-2's were added to the roster in 1923, and in 1935–1936, the Virginian modernized six of them. One more, plus four of the earlier group, were rebuilt during 1947–1951 with integrally-cast frames and low-pressure cylinders, Worthington feedwater heaters and 250 psi. boiler pressure. These rebuilt articulateds were Numbers 701, 702, 703, 705 and 735. [H. K. Vollrath Collection]

During 1947, the Virginian acquired seven elderly USRA 2-8+8-2's from the Santa Fe system. They had been built for the Norfolk & Western in 1919, modified by the N&W in the mid-1930's, and then sold to the Santa Fe in 1943. [H. K. Vollrath Collection]

The Tennessee & North Carolina extended eastward from a lumber mill at Andrews, North Carolina, through the forested mountains to Hayesville. Its sole motive power, a second-hand 70-ton three-truck Shay of 1912 vintage, is seen here at the lumber mill prior to its unscheduled daily trip. [R. A. LeMassena]

The DM&IR's four 0-10-0's, inherited from the Duluth, Missabe & Northern and numbered 90–93, had been built in 1928 by Baldwin. They weighed 352,000 pounds and could exert a tractive effort of 78,000 pounds when sorting heavy cuts of ore cars in the yard at Proctor, Minnesota. [C. C. Tinkham]

During World War II, some of the 2-10+10-2's had been working between Roanoke and Victoria, Virginia, and 2-8+8-2's had been assigned between there and Norfolk. Neither locomotive could run fast enough; so, the VGN bought eight 2-6+6-6 locomotives in 1945 — close copies of the Chesapeake & Ohio monsters — to cover the whole distance in less time. Together with the 2-8-4's, they were taken out of service in 1957, but were stored until 1960, when the Norfolk & Western absorbed the Virginian. No. 906, after a complete overhaul in 1954, never ran another mile. [C. W. Jernstrom]

Because it was owned by the Atlantic Coast Line and Norfolk & Western, the Winston-Salem Southbound Railroad acquired locomotives from those two "parent" railroads. A pair of 2–8–0's, numbered 711 and 716, of 1904 vintage, and a single rebuilt 2–6+6–2, No. 400 (ex-1393), had come from the N&W. The ACL contributed a pair of old 2–8–2's, whose efforts were supplemented by two more bought from Baldwin in 1925. [H. K. Vollrath Collection, R. B. Carneal]

# Chapter VI

### *MISCELLANEOUS*
*Duluth, Missabe & Iron Range*
*U.S. Army Transportation Corps*

The Duluth, Missabe & Iron Range transported iron ore for its owner, U.S. Steel; and it became the final refuge for locomotives from other U.S. Steel railroads: 2-10-4's from the Bessemer & Lake Erie; 2-8-2's from the Elgin, Joliet & Eastern; and 0-10-2's from the Union Railroad. Steam power remained in service until long after most other railroads had converted to diesel-electric locomotives.

The U.S. Army established a railroad facility at its transportation school in Fort Eustis, Virginia. Steam-locomotive operation, maintainance, repair and reconstruction were taught at that location.

The DM&IR's 2-8+8-4's were capable of hauling 20,000-ton trains of iron ore with their 140,000-pound tractive effort. The engine alone weighed 700,000 pounds, which was surpassed only by the C&O 2-6+6-6 and UP 4-8+8-4 engines. On such heavy trains, it was customary for the locomotive to be cut off while taking water, because it was much easier to position the tender beneath the spout from the tank. [R. A. LeMassena]

Duluth, Missabe & Iron Range passenger trains between Duluth and Ely or Hibbing, Minnesota, were pulled by eight 1913-model 4-6-2's, which Baldwin built for the railroad's two ancestors, the DM&N and the D&IR. No. 402, departing from Duluth with three U.S. Mail cars behind its tender, was an ex-Duluth, Missabe & Northern engine. [C. W. Burns]

Only half of the DM&N's 51 2-8-0's became DM&IR locomotives. One of the later ones, No. 347, from Baldwin in 1907, is seen at work in the Proctor Yard. This engine managed to survive and became the only one to have been preserved. [C. W. Burns]

Ten 0-8-0's and four 0-10-0's were needed to shuffle long-and-heavy cuts of ore cars at Proctor, Minnesota, the mainline terminal. Both engines were Baldwin products of 1917 and 1928, constructed for the DM&N. Note that both have dual airpumps and insulated smokeboxes. [C. W. Burns, C. W. Jernstrom]

The Duluth & Iron Range contributed 12 2-8-2's to the DM&IR in 1930, but in 1948, the Elgin, Joliet & Eastern — also owned by U.S. Steel Corporation — sent 26 more to the DM&IR, the last of which was No. 1337, built in 1930. By 1961, only a few remained in service. [H. K. Vollrath Collection, C. W. Burns]

In 1949, the DM&IR received nine unusual locomotives — 0-10-2's — from the Union Railroad, another U.S. Steel subsidiary. The only engines of that wheel arrangement newly constructed, by Baldwin in 1936 and 1939, they were put to work hauling ore cars between Proctor and the ship docks at Duluth. [I. W. Saunders]

Only the Southern valve gear would make one suspicious the 2-10-2 No. 510 was actually one of the USRA standard locomotives received by the DM&N in 1919. Since that time, the trailing truck had been replaced; sand boxes had been added to the pilot deck; the smokebox had been jacketed; and the tender's coal bunker had been modified. [C. W. Burns]

Another U.S. Steel railroad, the Bessemer & Lake Erie, had used heavy booster-equipped 2–10–4's, built by American and Baldwin between 1937 and 1943, and replaced them with diesel-electric locomotives in 1951. They were then sent to the DM&IR, where they hauled ore trains between Proctor and the docks at Duluth. Not only were they heavier than the old 2–8+8–2 Mallets; but also — with the booster operating — they equalled the articulated's 110,000-pound tractive effort. [C. W. Jernstrom]

To haul its 14,000-ton trains of iron ore the DM&IR bought 18 enormous 2-8+8-4's in 1941–1943. With an engine and tender weight of more than 1.1-million pounds and a tractive effort of 140,000 pounds, they were among the heaviest and most powerful steam locomotives ever produced. Because they were erected during the winter, when the DM&IR did not need them, Baldwin delivered them to the Denver & Rio Grande Western, which was short of motive power, to move World War II traffic. No. 225 is seen hauling a freight train south of Denver in December of 1942. [O. C. Perry]

Between the years 1910 and 1917, Baldwin delivered 12 compound-expansion 2–8+8–2's to the DM&N. The last five were rebuilt to single-expansion in the railroad's shops during 1929–1937, and no two were alike, all of them differing in airpumps, feedwater heaters and steam piping. After the monstrous 2–8+8–4's were received in 1941–1943, they were reassigned to Proctor-Duluth ore-train duties, and all were scrapped soon after the 2–10–4's arrived. [Both views: D. A. Somerville Collection]

Numbers 610 and 611 of the U.S. Army Transportation Corps were almost unknown locomotives, both of 2-8-0 wheel arrangement. The 610, built by Baldwin-Lima-Hamilton in 1952, was the last commercially-built reciprocating steam locomotive for a domestic railroad. It has been preserved and restored to operating condition. No. 611 emerged from Baldwin's plant in 1943. After the war, it was returned to the U.S.A., and was rebuilt with poppet valves by Vulcan in 1950, and remained in service at Fort Eustis, Virginia, until the mid-1950's. [H. K. Vollrath Collection]

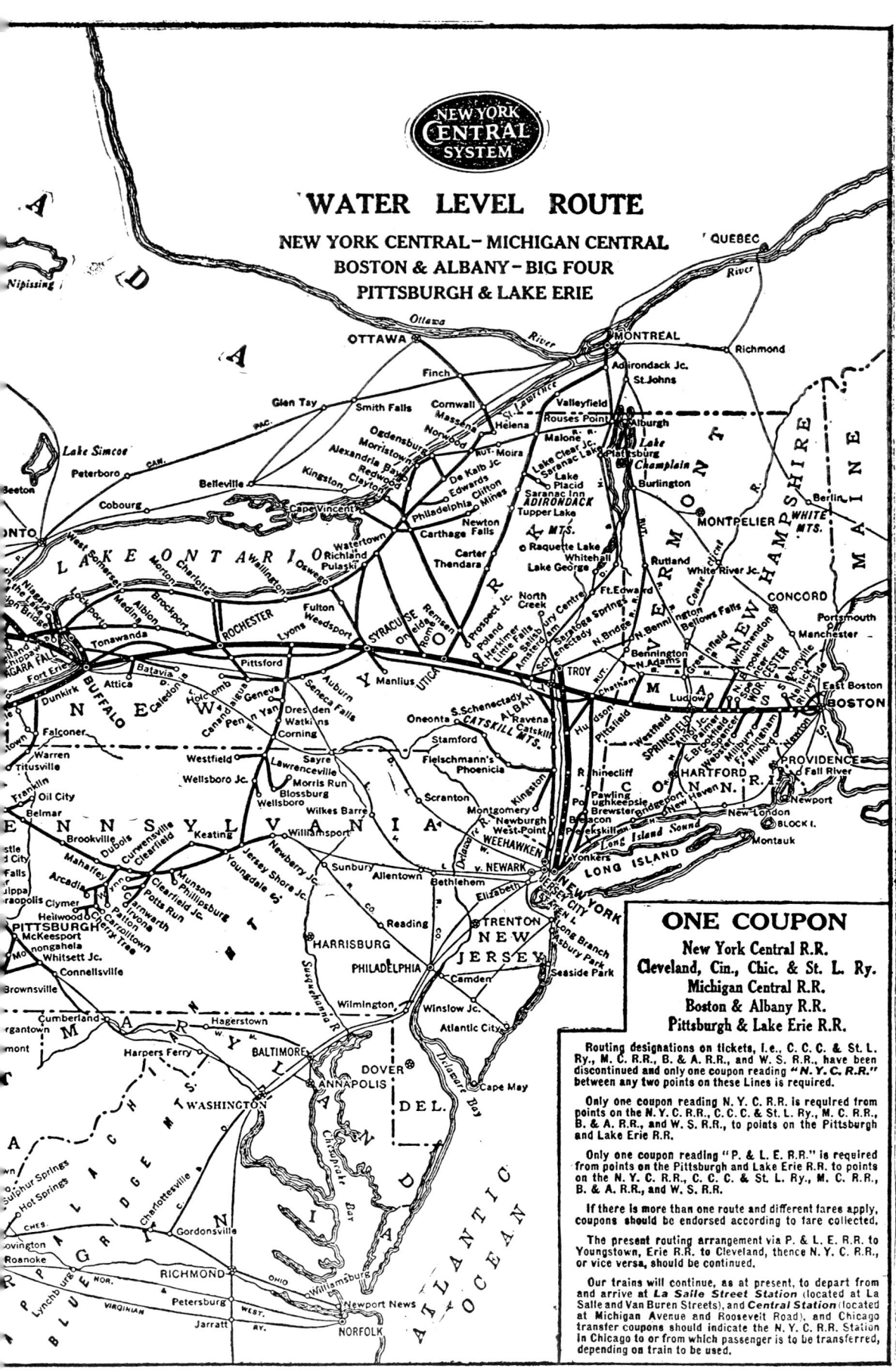

# COMMENTARY —

**WHILE ASSEMBLING THE PHOTOGRAPHS** for this book, and writing their captions, the author was impressed with two intriguing thoughts: that (1) there were a large number of second-hand locomotives, and (2) a great magnitude of modifications had taken place, as well as an incredible amount of re-building, apart from the construction of entire locomotives, in the railroads' own shops. Very nearly all of the 50 railroads included in this work performed modification or reconstruction, and no less than 10 built or erected complete locomotives on "home premises." Certainly, the output of the Norfolk & Western and the Pennsylvania was comparable with that of the major builders, American, Baldwin and Lima.

Modifications included such items as power reversing, feedwater heaters, lightweight rods, piston valves, valve gear, boosters, air pumps, stokers, oil-coal conversions, front-end throttles, disc drivers and one-piece trailing trucks. Rebuilding embraced such items as firebox conversions, new boilers, cast beds with integral cylinders and valve chambers, roller bearings, superheaters, compound- to single-expansion conversions, wheel-arrangement conversions and new tenders. During World War II, due to restrictions, some railroads "rebuilt" an existing engine by salvaging a single boiler ring, then constructing an otherwise completely new locomotive around it. The Illinois Central performed so much boiler and machinery swapping that only an expert could keep track of the multiple conversions.

Despite the wholesale scrapping of steam locomotives following World War II, a great many steam locomotives survived the mechanical massacre, and they have been preserved as static exhibits or in operative condition. There may be perhaps 2,000 of them, some of which are listed in the tabulation below. Locations are not shown because they change so frequently. (Current information for all preserved locomotives is contained in *The Steam Locomotive Directory of North America* (Transportation Trails, 9698 West Judson Road, Polo, Illinois 61064).

In the two volumes of *American Steam,* 86 railroads are listed; of these, 63 have preserved steam locomotives, represented by 43 wheel arrangements. Eleven of these are articulateds, ranging from 2-6+6-2 to 4-8+8-4 Mallets, plus three varieties of geared articulateds. Nearly all are standard gauge; a few are three-foot gauge. There are tank engines, rack-and-pinion, steam storage, three-cylinder and compound-expansion locomotives, truly an amazing variety. The following examples are particularly noteworthy:

**AT&SF:** 0-4-0, 0-6-0, 2-6-2, 4-6-2, the most powerful 4-6-4, 2-8-0, 4-8-4, 2-10-2, the most powerful 2-10-4.
**C&O:** 0-6-0, 4-6-0, 4-6-4, 2-8-0, the most powerful 2-8-4, 4-8-4, 2-6+6-2 (the last commercially built steam engine for a common-carrier railroad), 2-6+6-6 (the most powerful and heaviest steam locomotive).
**D&RGW:** narrow-gauge 4-6-0, 2-8-0, 2-8-2.
**DM&IR:** the most powerful 2-8+8-4.
**Mt.W:** 0-2 = 2-0 (the only operating rack-and-pinion locomotives east of the Mississippi).
**PRR:** a very wide variety of wheel arrangements, 2-2-2T, 0-4-0, 2-4-0, 4-4-0, 4-4-2, 0-6-0, 2-6-0, 4-6-0, 4-6-2, 2-8-0, 2-8-2, 4-8-2, 0-10-0T, 2-10-0.
**PP&L:** 0-8-0F (biggest two-cylinder steam-storage engine).
**N&W:** the most powerful 4-8-4, 2-6+6-4 (the most powerful operating locomotive), 2-8+8-2 (the only existing specimens of this very common wheel arrangement).
**SP:** the largest variety, 4-2-4T, 0-4-0T, 4-4-0, 4-4-2, 0-6-0, 2-6-0, 2-6-2T, 4-6-0, 4-6-2, 2-8-0, 2-8-2, 4-8-4, 2-10-2, 4-10-2 (three-cylinder), 2-8+8-4 (cab-forward).
**UP:** 4-4-0, 0-6-0, 4-6-2, 2-8-0, 2-8-2, 4-8-4, 2-10-2, the only 4-12-2 (three-cylinder), 4-6+6-4 (the only one operating), 4-8+8-4 (the only ones of that wheel arrangement).
**USATC:** 2-8-0 (the last steam engine produced by a commercial builder).
**WM:** a three-truck Shay (the last and biggest existing geared locomotive).

It is particularly regrettable that many notable examples of steam locomotives have not been preserved. The articulated, especially the Mallets, have suffered the greatest attrition. None of the Baldwin flexible-beam engines have survived; likewise, the double-Fairlie engine, though one single-Fairlie locomotive exists today. The geared articulateds, Shay, Climax and Heisler, have survived because they were used by logging and mining companies, which saw no need to convert to diesel-electric locomotion. Of the smallest Mallets, only one, a 2-4+4-2, exists; there are none of the 2-6+6-0, only a few of the most common 2-6+6-2, and none of the odd 2-6+8-0 type. A single 2-6+6-4 has been preserved, plus a couple of 4-6+6-4's, and two of the gigantic 2-6+6-6's. The 2-8+8-0 and 2-10+10-2 have vanished completely; only two 2-8+8-2's (compound) still exist, along with three 2-8+8-4's, and a few 4-8+8-4's. No example of the huge duplex locomotives remains, though some tiny geared engines are still being operated. Surprisingly, however, almost every variety of non-articulated wheel arrangement can be seen somewhere.

Many notable steam locomotives are extinct, as indicated in the following listing:
Modern 0-8-0 – P&LE, N&W, C&O.
Heavy 4-6-2 – CNJ, DL&W, Erie, P&LE, C&O, CStPM&O.
Powerful 4-8-4 – NYC, C&O, MP, D&RGW, NP.
Modern 4-8-2 – MP, SL-SF, B&O.
Early 2-8-4 – B&A, B&M, Erie, IC.
Most 4-6-4 – NYC.
Big 2-10-4 – C&O, PRR.
Most 4-8-4 – CRI&P.
Heaviest 4-6+6-4 – D&RGW, NP.
Simple 2-8+8-2 – D&RGW, GN, WP.
First/last 2-8+8-4 – NP, B&O.
Biggest 2-10-0 – L&NE, WM.
Largest 2-8-2 – GN.

All that can be said is that the railroads were is such a hurry to become 100-percent non-steam that serviceable locomotives were set aside or scrapped without any consideration of preservation. At least, we can be grateful for the preservation of those which exist today, so that we can appreciate these wonderful machines in a way which no photograph or scale model could possibly approximate. It is even more fortuitous that many steam locomotives are still being operated, thus appealing to our senses of sight, sound, feeling, smell and — yes — even taste.